RODALE'S
SUCCESSFUL ORGANIC GARDENING™
PRUNING

RODALE'S
SUCCESSFUL ORGANIC GARDENING™
PRUNING

KRIS MEDIC

Rodale Press, Emmaus, Pennsylvania

Our Mission

We publish books that empower people's lives.

RODALE BOOKS

If you have any questions or comments concerning this book, please write to:

Rodale Press
Book Readers' Service
33 East Minor Street
Emmaus, PA 18098

Library of Congress Cataloging-in-Publication Data

Medic, Kris.
    Pruning / Kris Medic.
       p. cm. — (Rodale's successful organic gardening)
    "A Kevin Weldon production" —T.p. verso.
    Includes index.
    ISBN 0–87596–661–6 hardcover — ISBN 0–87596–662–4 paperback
    1. Pruning. I. Title. II. Series.
S8125.M42 1995
635'.0442—dc20   94–26692
                           CIP

Produced by Mandarin Offset, Hong Kong
Printed in Hong Kong on acid-free paper ∞

Rodale Press Staff:
    Executive Editor, Home and Garden Books: Margaret Lydic Balitas
    Managing Editor, Gardening Books: Barbara W. Ellis
    Editor: Nancy J. Ondra
    Copy Editor: Carolyn R. Mandarano
    Editor-in-Chief: William Gottlieb

Produced for Rodale Press by Weldon Russell Pty Ltd
107 Union Street, North Sydney NSW 2060, Australia
a member of the Weldon International Group of Companies

    Publisher: Elaine Russell
    General Manager: Karen Hammial
    Managing Editor: Ariana Klepac
    Editor: Libby Frederico
    Editorial Assistant: Cassandra Sheridan
    Horticultural Consultant: Cheryl Maddocks
    Copy Editor: Yani Silvana
    Designer: Rowena Sheppard
    Picture Researcher: Elizabeth Connolly
    Illustrators: Tony Brit-Lewis, Barbara Rodanska, Jan Smith
    Macintosh Layout Artist: Rachel Smith
    Indexer: Michael Wyatt
    Production Manager: Dianne Leddy

A KEVIN WELDON PRODUCTION

Distributed in the book trade by St. Martin's Press

2 4 6 8 10 9 7 5 3 1 hardcover
2 4 6 8 10 9 7 5 3 1 paperback

Opposite: Japanese maple (*Acer japonica*)
Front cover: Forsythia (*Forsythia* x *intermedia spectabilis*)
Half title: *Sorbus* 'Sunshine'
Opposite title page: *Clematis* 'Perle D'azur'
Opposite contents: Plum 'Victoria'
Contents: *Camellia* 'Mathiotiana' (top left)
Back cover: *Photinia* (top), cherries (center)

CONTENTS

INTRODUCTION

It's been said that people who plant trees are affirming their faith in the future. The same could be said of those who have the vision, foresight, and commitment to guide and train their trees—or anything that they plant—for that future. Whether you're anticipating centuries, decades, or just the end-of-summer harvest, you express your vision for the future each time you head out with a sharp pair of shears. Pruners as visionaries? You bet!

But even though you may be confident in the future, you may not be confident in the pruning that you need to do in the here and now. When you actually go out to prune, it's easy to become overwhelmed by all the choices you need to make. *When* is the best time to prune? *What* should you prune out, and *how much* should you cut off? *Why* did the plant produce loads of watersprouts last time you pruned, and *how* can you avoid that problem this time?

This guide will give you the answers you need to prune all kinds of landscape plants competently and fearlessly. You'll even find out how well-timed pruning can actually reduce the regular maintenance your plants will need as they mature.

With experience, you'll discover that you can often predict a plant's response to pruning this way or that. Even if you make a mistake—or if you are reclaiming a plant from someone else's mistakes—you'll learn lots and gain confidence when you discover that pruning mistakes are rarely fatal. Soon you'll be able to amaze your friends, family, and neighbors with your pruning savvy. You may even startle them with an occasional feat of derring-do, such as cutting an overgrown shrub completely to the ground for renovation pruning. Others may think that what you're doing is mysterious or complicated—or foolish, before they see the results—but you'll know better.

Whether you're growing shade trees, flowering trees, shrubs, roses, vines, or fruit trees, pruning can be a tremendously satisfying and rewarding aspect of gardening. Your well-pruned plants will produce more flowers, more fruit, or more colorful stems or leaves—whatever it is that you're growing them for in the first place. You'll discover a keen sense of satisfaction and accomplishment as you develop your pruning skills using the techniques covered in *Rodale's Successful Organic Gardening: Pruning*. And—better yet—you'll start seeing results right away as you begin to prune with confidence.

What could be more rewarding than a landscape full of beautiful flowers, majestic trees, colorful shrubs, and sweet fruits? With proper pruning, all of your plants can grow and produce to their potential.

How to Use This Book

Thoughtful, careful pruning helps you to get the best from your landscape plants. Your trees, shrubs, vines, herbs, flowers, and fruits will flourish and prosper when you add pruning to your repertoire of gardening talents. *Rodale's Successful Organic Gardening: Pruning* is your guide to knowing when, what, and how to prune effectively.

Before you grab a pair of pruners and head out to the yard, take a few minutes to review "Pruning Basics," starting on page 12. This section will help you to understand the basic goals that apply to pruning and which ones apply to your task at hand. Knowing when to prune is just as important as making the right cuts. "Pruning Basics" will guide you in making those decisions so you'll be making less work for yourself, rather than more. There's also a short list of basic pruning terms and a review of pruning tools: What you use them for, what to look for in a new tool, and how to use them safely.

"Pruning Shrubs and Hedges," starting on page 24, leads off with specifics on pruning strategies for keeping shrubs healthy and happy in their allotted space. You'll find ways to keep your flowering plants full of flowers, your foundation plants from covering the windows, and your evergreen hedge leafy and full to the ground. You'll learn how to renovate an old overgrown shrub and how to create a graceful, low-maintenance hedge. You'll even find a list of low- and slow-growing shrubs and hedge plants that stay in great shape with minimal pruning.

Trees to prune? Turn to "Pruning Trees," starting on page 54. You'll find out how to prune your young trees to a sound, sturdy structure that will last for life. Follow the checklist for inspecting mature trees to help you spot possible problems before serious damage occurs. If your mature tree does need corrective pruning, you'll learn how to choose a reputable arborist or tree service that can help.

"Pruning Vines," starting on page 84, will guide you in finding the right vine for the support you have or the right support for that vine you bought. You'll find out how to train and attach your vine to its supports, the best ways to prune it, and even how to rejuvenate an old overgrown vine.

"Pruning Fruits, Nuts, and Berries," starting on page 100, is a must if you're gardening for such homegrown delicacies as apples, peaches, pears, cherries, walnuts, and many other wonderful edibles. You'll find easy-to-follow instructions on how to train strong, productive fruit trees and how to keep small fruits like grapevines and raspberries under control and producing abundantly. You'll even find out how good pruning can help to discourage devastating diseases like fire blight.

Flower gardeners won't want to miss "Pruning Roses, Flowers, and Herbs," starting on page 132. A section on rose pruning basics will show you what to do and explain how your pruning can maximize bloom and minimize disease on any type of rose. You'll also find lots of tips and techniques you can use to coax more blooms out of annuals and perennials and more tasty leaves out of your herbs.

If you like to prune and you aren't shy about showing off your talents, spend some time with "Special Pruning Projects," starting on page 146. Here you'll find pointers on several kinds of fun and fanciful techniques, including bonsai, espalier, and topiary.

Plant-by-Plant Guides

Once you've read the chapters that apply to your plants, you'll have a good basic understanding of how pruning works. But when you're ready to go out and prune, you'll want a quick-reference guide to remind you of the basic cuts you need to make. This book includes four quick-reference sections: "Guide to Shrubs and Hedges," starting on page 32; "Guide to Trees," starting on page 62; "Guide to Vines," starting on page 92; and "Guide to Fruiting Plants," starting on page 120.

In total, these plant-by-plant guides offer specific pruning information for over 124 different plants.

Each entry features a color photograph for easy identification of the plant, followed by a description, basic growing information, and details of when and how to prune. If you're looking for a specific plant, look it up in the appropriate section under its botanical name. Only know the common name? Simply look it up in the index and you'll find the botanical name listed with it. The diagram below helps explain what you'll find on these practical pages.

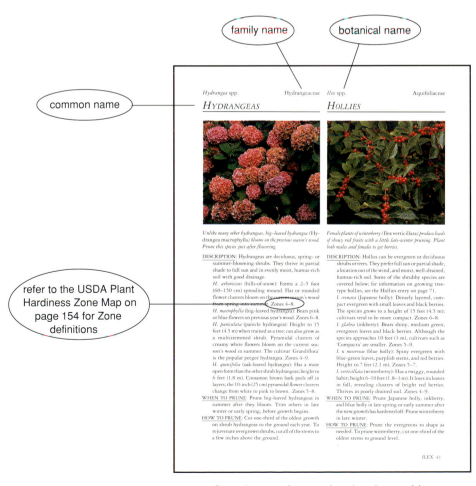

family name

botanical name

common name

refer to the USDA Plant Hardiness Zone Map on page 154 for Zone definitions

Hydrangea spp.   Hydrangeaceae

HYDRANGEAS

Unlike many other hydrangeas, big-leaved hydrangea (Hydrangea macrophylla) blooms on the previous season's wood. Prune this species just after flowering.

DESCRIPTION: Hydrangeas are deciduous, spring- or summer-blooming shrubs. They thrive in partial shade to full sun and in evenly moist, humus-rich soil with good drainage.

H. arborescens (hills-of-snow): Forms a 2–5 foot (60–150 cm) spreading mound. Flat or rounded flower clusters bloom on the current season's wood from spring into summer. Zones 4–8.

H. macrophylla (big-leaved hydrangea): Bears pink or blue flowers on previous year's wood. Zones 6–8.

H. paniculata (panicle hydrangea): Height to 15 feet (4.5 m) when trained as a tree; can also grow as a multistemmed shrub. Pyramidal clusters of creamy white flowers bloom on the current season's wood in summer. The cultivar 'Grandiflora' is the popular peegee hydrangea. Zones 4–9.

H. quercifolia (oak-leaved hydrangea): Has a more open form than the other shrub hydrangeas; height to 6 feet (1.8 m). Cinnamon brown bark peels off in layers; the 10-inch (25 cm) pyramidal flower clusters change from white to pink to brown. Zones 5–8.

WHEN TO PRUNE: Prune big-leaved hydrangeas in summer after they bloom. Trim others in late winter or early spring, before growth begins.

HOW TO PRUNE: Cut one-third of the oldest growth on shrub hydrangeas to the ground each year. To rejuvenate overgrown shrubs, cut all of the stems to a few inches above the ground.

Ilex spp.   Aquifoliaceae

HOLLIES

Female plants of winterberry (Ilex verticillata) produce loads of showy red fruits with a little late-winter pruning. Plant both males and females to get berries.

DESCRIPTION: Hollies can be evergreen or deciduous shrubs or trees. They prefer full sun or partial shade, a location out of the wind, and moist, well-drained, humus-rich soil. Some of the shrubby species are covered below; for information on growing tree-type hollies, see the Hollies entry on page 71.

I. crenata (Japanese holly): Densely layered, compact evergreen with small leaves and black berries. The species grows to a height of 15 feet (4.5 m); cultivars tend to be more compact. Zones 6–8.

I. glabra (inkberry): Bears shiny, medium green, evergreen leaves and black berries. Although the species approaches 10 feet (3 m), cultivars such as 'Compacta' are smaller. Zones 5–9.

I. x meserveae (blue holly): Spiny evergreen with blue-green leaves, purplish stems, and red berries. Height to 7 feet (2.1 m). Zones 5–7.

I. verticillata (winterberry): Has a twiggy, rounded habit; height 6–10 feet (1.8–3 m). It loses its leaves in fall, revealing clusters of bright red berries. Thrives in poorly drained soil. Zones 4–9.

WHEN TO PRUNE: Prune Japanese holly, inkberry, and blue holly in late spring or early summer after the new growth has hardened off. Prune winterberry in late winter.

HOW TO PRUNE: Prune the evergreens to shape as needed. To prune winterberry, cut one-third of the oldest stems to ground level.

ILEX 41

Sample page from a plant by plant guide.

PRUNING BASICS

Careful pruning can bring out the best in any plant and the best in any landscape. When you prune with the right tools at the right time, your plants will naturally be more beautiful and more healthy. As a bonus, properly pruned plants will require less—not more—maintenance with each passing year.

Yes, it's surprising but true: you actually *can* reduce your landscape maintenance if you prune regularly. Think of it this way: Have you ever faced a completely overgrown landscape and put in endless hours of pruning and related labor to get it into shape? When you've had an experience like that once, it's tempting to put off the task again for a long time. Then you end up back where you started, with weeks of labor ahead of you. But what if you were to work those various pruning tasks into a year-round schedule, one that broke things down into doable chunks? There would be no more herculean efforts to reclaim your landscape from sprawling or overgrown plants—just a little routine trimming here and there throughout the year. It's possible and a lot easier than you might think!

Making pruning a regular part of garden maintenance is the first step to becoming a great pruner. The next step is knowing when and why you're pruning so you can plan a practical pruning strategy. Then you're ready to learn the basic pruning techniques you'll use to prune all kinds of plants, from roses and shrubs to vines and fruit trees. This chapter covers the basic skills that will get you started, including setting pruning goals, knowing when to prune, making basic pruning cuts, and choosing the right tools and supplies to make your pruning a pleasure.

One of the best ways to become a confident pruner is to practice the techniques you learn in this chapter. Once you begin to use these skills as a way of *looking* at your plants—not just as a way of *treating* them—you'll be well on your way to satisfying and successful pruning. You'll know what results to expect from various methods, and you'll be able to anticipate problems before they happen. Best of all, you'll be training your plants in harmony with their natural inclinations, so they'll be free to develop to their potential. So protect the investment you've made in your landscape—learn how to help your plants be the best they can be!

When you know the right way to do it, pruning your trees, shrubs, vines, and flowers can be a pleasure instead of a pain. And by pruning at the right time, you will get the best show of flowers, fruit, and foliage.

Prune with a Purpose

"How will I know when I'm finished?" is a common—and understandable—question often asked by people who are pruning for the first time. Keeping a clear goal in mind is one way experienced pruners avoid that uncertainty and make steady progress in their pruning tasks. "Today I'll remove all of the dead wood from this crab apple," or "This morning we'll remove one-third of the oldest stems on that abelia" are the kinds of purpose statements that we all should be able to make before reaching for the pruning tools.

Part of establishing an effective goal is knowing *why* you are pruning. Only then can you decide *how* to go about it. Below is a summary of the basic purposes you might consider when planning a pruning strategy. Once you know what you want to accomplish, move on to "Know When to Prune" on page 16 to plan the timing.

Keeping Plants Healthy and Attractive

The pruning jobs you do to maintain a plant's health and appearance are the ones that take the least time and have the biggest payoff. To keep plants looking their best, you will want to:

- Remove dead, dying, or diseased wood.
- Cut out unwanted growth, like watersprouts and sucker shoots.
- Prune out crossing or rubbing stems.
- Thin out stems to open the plant to light and air.
- Remove any overly long or awkward-looking shoots.

All kinds of trees, shrubs, and vines benefit from this kind of pruning on a regular basis. These basic steps

If you spot rubbing branches, prune one out. The rubbing can create wounds, which are prime targets for pests.

will quickly become an automatic part of all the pruning that you do throughout the year.

Controlling Plant Size

The next thing you may need to consider is pruning to control a plant's size. If you've carefully planned your landscape and spaced the plants properly, they may be able to grow for years without this kind of pruning. Sooner or later, though, every gardener faces at least one overgrown landscape plant that needs help. Things to look for include:

- Plants that you need to keep a certain size, like a hedge or a shrub in a foundation planting.
- Plants that are crowded into other plants.
- Stems that are leaning into paths, walkways, or doorways, making it difficult or dangerous to pass by.
- Plants that are simply too big for the space you have.

Allow plenty of room at planting time so your plants can spread without crowding. You'll have less pruning to do, and your plants will stay healthier, too.

Pruning out old stems each year promotes vigorous new growth.

Many roses benefit from regular pruning to encourage new flowering growth and to thin crowded leaves and stems.

When you're trying to keep a hedge or other formally trimmed plant under control, prune as often as needed to keep it the right size and shape. In other cases, the approach you take will depend on the growth habit of the plant. If just one or two branches are a problem, simply cutting them out as you spot them may be the answer. If plants are overgrown and crowding into each other, the situation calls for more drastic measures. Some plants (including many shrubs and vines) will resprout into a smaller, bushier form if you cut the old stems back to a few inches above the ground. Evergreens and deciduous trees, however, don't respond well to this treatment. If space is really a problem, consider removing the plant altogether and replacing it with something else. The individual plant entries throughout this book will help you decide if renovation or removal is the answer.

Keep in mind that buying only the plants you have room for and allowing ample room for each to develop will go a long way toward minimizing this kind of pruning. Read the plant tag, ask the nursery staff, or look in a reference book to find out how big you can expect a given plant to get as it matures. When you take the plant home, make sure you give it the space it needs without crowding it; the plant will be more beautiful, and you'll have less pruning to do!

Improving Flowering and Fruiting

Good pruning is the most important step you can take to enhance the performance of flowering and fruiting plants. This kind of pruning involves:

- Thinning cuts to remove crowded stems and to open a plant to light and air.
- Removing old wood to encourage vigorous new growth and more flowers.
- Taking out dead and unproductive wood.

Making this kind of pruning a regular part of a plant's seasonal care is a sensible and satisfying approach. Removing dead or unproductive wood will help direct the plant's energy to where it does the most good—into developing healthy shoots and strong roots.

Reducing Hazards

If you have shade trees on your property, you'll need to consider pruning for hazard control. Hazard reduction consists of:

- Removing narrow or weak branch crotches, dead wood, and crossing or rubbing limbs.
- Thinning out branches to reduce wind or snow loading and to balance the crown.
- Providing cabling, bracing, or lightning protection on mature trees.

Careful pruning on young trees is the most effective way to avoid problems in the future. The best hazard-reduction pruning on a shade tree happens during the first years after planting. Just a few minutes each year with hand pruners and loppers on a young plant can eliminate virtually hours of costly professional aerial work on an older, untrained tree.

Creating Unusual Plant Forms

As you gain experience in pruning, you may decide to experiment with different methods to create interesting plant shapes. Specialized techniques like bonsai, topiary, and espalier use pruning to change the natural shape of a plant to serve a specific purpose. To learn more about these methods, see "Special Pruning Projects," starting on page 146.

Regular pruning on apples and other fruit trees will promote sturdy branches and a generous harvest.

Know When to Prune

The old adage "Do your pruning when the knife is sharp" reflects the generalist sense that there is really no bad time to prune. While there is wisdom in this, we also know that some seasons of the year are better than others for certain pruning tasks. Let your pruning be guided by your plants and your goal.

Rest assured that there truly is no bad time to remove dead, dying, or broken branches. For other tasks, check the guidelines that follow and in the sections of this book that pertain to the specific plants you wish to prune.

Pruning in the Dormant Season

In general, dormant pruning tends to have an invigorating effect on your plants. Removing top growth during the dormant season leaves the plant with proportionately greater root and energy reserves. When the growing season begins again, there's plenty of energy to support new growth on the remaining branches.

Dormant-season pruning has many benefits for you as well. To start with, the absence of foliage gives you a better view of the work at hand, so you can work more quickly. You'll also have less material to chip, compost, or haul away. As you gain pruning experience, you'll come to know how the presence of foliage can really slow down or belabor a pruning task, and you'll greatly appreciate the advantages of dormant-season pruning.

If you are hiring a contractor to do some of your pruning work, the very same considerations come into play. Tree for tree, dormant-season pruning takes less time and fewer resources, meaning reduced charges for time and materials as compared with the same job done during the growing season. Moreover, the dormant season tends to be a slower time for most arborists, so it's not unusual to see reduced rates and to receive more personal attention during the winter months.

The dormant season is also the time to trim flowering shrubs that will bloom on new (current-season) wood. Abelias (*Abelia*

Birches, maples, and several other trees may bleed sap in spring after dormant pruning; wait until summer to prune.

spp.), orange-eye butterfly bush (*Buddleia davidii*), bluebeard (*Caryopteris* x *clandonensis*), hibiscus (*Hibiscus* spp.), and many other shrubs fall into this category. Pruning during the dormant season removes much of the old wood and invigorates these plants, causing them to bloom and fruit more abundantly. If you develop this pruning habit, you will never have a problem with these shrubs becoming overgrown—size control is built right in!

One possible disadvantage of dormant pruning is that the pruning wounds won't really start to heal until plants start active growth in spring. When your schedule permits, try to concentrate dormant-season pruning jobs in late winter. That way, you'll get the advantages of dormant pruning, and your plants will soon be on their way to active growth and recovery.

Summer-flowering shrubs bloom on new stems; prune them back in spring.

You can promote dense growth on evergreens by pinching the new growth.

Azaleas and rhododendrons bloom on the previous season's growth, so it's best to prune them just after flowering.

Pruning during the Growing Season

Late spring and summer are also good times to prune, depending on your plants and the results you want. In general, pruning during the growing season tends to decrease plant vigor, since you're taking away growth into which the plant has already put a significant amount of energy. This effect can be a plus if you're trying to keep a plant a certain size (like a hedge) or to minimize sucker formation. If you wish to suppress growth or reduce the natural suckering response of a fruit tree, consider scheduling your pruning job for summer.

Early summer is also a great time to prune lilacs, forsythias, and other flowering shrubs that bloomed on the previous year's wood. Wait until after flowering to prune, but don't wait too long! The exact amount of time you have can vary from plant to plant, but it's usually safe to figure on having a month to prune after the plants stop blooming. After that, they will begin to form flower buds for the next year, and belated pruning will remove next year's flowers.

Evergreen shrubs and trees respond best to pruning when they are in active growth. Spring is a good time to trim the "candles" of new growth on pines and similar plants. Summer is the season for trimming other evergreen trees, shrubs, and hedges.

Maples, dogwoods, yellowwood (*Cladrastis lutea*), and some other trees are known to "bleed" sap if you prune them in late winter or early spring when sap is rising. While this response isn't harmful, it can be unsightly or unsettling. Consider summer or fall pruning on these kinds of plants. (You'll find a more complete list in "Bleeding Trees" on page 57.)

If fungal and bacterial plant diseases like dogwood anthracnose, oak wilt, and fire blight are a problem in your area, you'll need to keep them in mind when scheduling your pruning. Where these diseases are present, it's usually best to avoid pruning during the wet spring weather that favors them. Wait until the drier weather of summer or fall to prune most disease-prone trees and shrubs; even then, consider disinfecting your pruning equipment as part of the task.

Pruning toward the end of the growing season always brings the danger of frost damage to any resulting new growth. Be sure to finish your late-season pruning tasks in plenty of time for any new growth to harden off (become adapted to the cold). There are no set guidelines to tell you exactly when to stop, but midsummer is a good rule of thumb. Once cold weather settles in after several frosts, you can start pruning again.

Pruning Timetable

Here are some guidelines to help you plan your pruning schedule, based on the plants you have and the results you want to achieve.

Winter and Early Spring
- Remove dead, dying, or broken branches.
- Prune to invigorate deciduous trees, shrubs, and vines.
- Cut back stems to rejuvenate overgrown deciduous shrubs and vines.
- Prune out old stems on flowering shrubs that bloom on new growth.

Late Spring and Summer
- Remove any dead, dying, diseased, or broken branches as you see them.
- Cut off suckers and watersprouts.
- Pinch stems or rub off buds as needed.
- Prune plants as needed if you want to reduce their vigor.
- Trim trees that "bleed."
- Prune flowering shrubs that bloom on older wood within a month after flowering is over.
- Prune evergreen trees, shrubs, and hedges while they are actively growing.
- Trim disease-prone plants during dry weather to reduce the chance of infection.

Master the Basic Cuts

An understanding of the basic cuts, terms, and tools used in pruning will get you on the right track and pruning like a pro.

Thinning

A thinning cut removes a limb at its point of origin, either at a branch collar or at ground level. You'll use thinning cuts to:

- Remove suckers, watersprouts, and other unwanted growth.
- Take out damaged, crossing, or rubbing branches.
- Open the center of a plant to light and air.
- Reduce the weight load of wind, rain, snow, ice, or of the branches themselves.
- Open desirable views through plants.

By removing old, injured, or unwanted branches with thinning cuts, you help to improve flowering and fruiting and to reduce insect and disease problems.

Heading

Heading cuts take off stem tips. Their main effect on plants is to encourage new growth lower on the stems. Since they remove the terminal buds, heading cuts cause

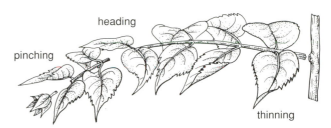

Pinching removes the shoot tip. Heading cuts trim shoots back to leaves or buds; thinning cuts remove whole shoots.

the remaining buds to break into growth, making the plant fuller. These kinds of cuts are commonly used for:

- Shearing formal hedges.
- Encouraging compact, bushy growth on shrubs as well as on many herbs and flowers.

Selective Heading   A selective heading cut removes a branch back to a side bud or shoot. This kind of heading gives a more natural effect and is healthier for the plant, since it doesn't leave stubs or cut leaves.

When cutting back to a bud, select one that points in the direction you would like the new growth to go. A bud that points inward or toward other branches will lead to crossing or rubbing limbs later on. On alternately branched plants, cut to about $\frac{1}{4}$ inch (6 mm) above a bud, at a slant away from the bud. Oppositely branched plants have their buds in pairs, so make a flat cut. You also have the option here of rubbing off one of the buds in the pair if it seems to be headed in an undesirable direction.

Non-selective Heading   This kind of cut removes all the branch tips that are level with the plane where the shears make the cut. Non-selective heading, also known as shearing, is easiest and most effective on soft, new growth, where the newly cut ends heal easily and form new buds toward the tip. This technique is what

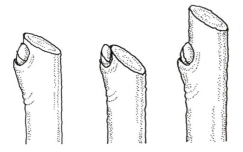

When pruning, make a sloped cut just above a bud (left). Avoid cutting too close (center) or leaving a stub (right).

Thinning cuts help to retain a plant's natural branching structure and open up dense, crowded growth.

Non-selective heading—also known as shearing—is best saved for trimming formal hedges and topiary.

Pruning Terms

Just like any skill, pruning has its own terminology. We've tried to keep the jargon to a minimum, but there are some terms that you really need to understand to be an effective pruner. Here are definitions for some common pruning terms that you'll find used throughout this book.

Apical dominance: The condition in most plants where the tip bud grows more strongly than the buds lower on the stem. If you cut off the top bud, apical dominance is lost and the remaining buds grow more quickly.

Branch collar: The zone where a branch meets a stem. The collar is usually easiest to see as a bulge at the base of a large branch, but even small branches have collars. When you make a pruning cut, always leave the collar; this is a site of rapid cell division and wound closure.

Callus: The scar tissue that naturally forms around wounds, such as pruning cuts, on woody plants.

Candle: The compact, expanding new growth that appears on pines, spruces, and firs in the spring.

Cane: A long, slender branch that usually originates directly from the roots.

Crotch: The angle formed between two branches or between a branch and the trunk.

Deadheading: The removal of spent flowers or unripe seedpods.

Lateral branch: Any branch growing from a larger branch.

Leader: The main, primary, or tallest vertical branch originating from the trunk of a tree.

Scaffold branches: The primary limbs that originate from the main trunk of a tree and form its structure.

Spur: A short, often thorn-like shoot that produces flowers, fruit, and leaves. Some spurs are permanent; some only live a few years. Landscape plants that have spurs include ginkgo, larch, some apples, and kiwi fruit.

Stub: An unsightly and soon-to-be-dead branch piece left when a cut was not made to a bud or originating branch.

Sucker shoot: An upright shoot growing from a root or graft union.

Watersprout: A vigorous upright branch that originates along another branch.

leader

lateral branch

stub

scaffold branch

watersprout

sucker

you'll use to maintain the smooth-clipped look of formal hedges. Be aware that once you shear a plant, you'll have to keep shearing it to maintain the shape; it's *not* a low-maintenance technique!

Pinching and Rubbing

Pinching and rubbing are underrated as pruning techniques, perhaps because they require no fancy tools—only your hands! Pinching, a common technique for training perennials and herbs, is also useful for training young vines, shrubs, and trees. A pinch is a heading cut, used only on very soft tissue. Pinching out stem tips is a handy technique for getting young growth to fill in lower on the stems. You'll find more details on this technique in "Pruning and Training Annuals and Perennials" on page 141.

Rubbing refers to rubbing off undesirable buds, such as sprouts on the trunk or scaffold branches of a fruit tree, or any young growth that seems to be heading in the wrong direction. You can brush off very soft buds with your fingertips; a fingernail can be more effective for slightly harder growth. If you're careful, you could even use a knife to flick off unwanted buds.

Both pinching and rubbing are time-savers for the busy gardener. Once you get good at spying growth that needs pinching or rubbing, you'll find yourself doing it on the spot and reducing future pruning time significantly.

Using sharp pruning tools that are suited to the task will make your job easier and keep plants in good shape.

Choose the Right Tools

As with so many tasks, the right tool for the job makes pruning more of a joy than a chore. Passionate pruners will enjoy investigating the many and various types of shears, saws, and related tools. Most gardeners, though, will need little more than hand pruners, loppers, and a small pruning saw. Consider the tips below when you're in the market for a tool, and look for the best features rather than the most expensive ones. Kept sharpened, oiled, and clean, most good-quality pruning tools will give a lifetime of service.

Hand Pruners

Use hand pruners to remove growth that's ³/₄ inch (18 mm) diameter and smaller. Choose bypass pruners over anvil-type pruners: The latter tend to crush stems, while the scissor action of the former makes a cleaner cut.

Ratchet-action hand pruners have become more available and may be worthwhile for people with limited strength in their hands. However, don't be tempted to use the extra power to cut pieces larger than the ³/₄-inch (18 mm) guideline; you may end up crushing or tearing the tissue left on the plant. You'll occasionally see orchardists or arborists using pneumatic pruners that are powered by an air compressor. This invention does help to reduce the fatigue of repetitive pruning tasks done all day long, but it can be dangerous if you're not properly trained in its use. The power of that air compressor can't tell the difference between a branch and your thumb, so one careless moment can have tragic results. In most cases, hand-powered tools are best for pruning jobs around the home.

Carrying pruners in your pocket can be tough on your clothes and on you, too, if you forget they are there! A holster for your hand pruners is a wonderful accessory because it keeps them comfortably close at hand. With pruners at the ready, you're more likely to make a cut when you see the need.

Loppers

If you find yourself using two hands to make a cut with your hand pruners, stop and reach for loppers. Loppers work best on cuts up to 1³/₄ inches (4.3 cm) in diameter. Choose wood handles (ash, preferably) over metal for better shock absorption, and pick bypass over anvil for the cutting mechanism. Also look for models with a rubber disk that functions as a shock absorber when the tool snaps closed. It won't take much pruning at all for you (and your back, neck, and shoulders) to appreciate this little, inexpensive feature.

As with hand pruners, consider ratchet mechanisms only if you have limited upper body strength and need all the help you can get to make a regular cut. Under most conditions, difficulty in making a cut may mean that your tool needs sharpening or that you're using the wrong tool. Simply applying more power will cause something to give—the tool, the plant, or you—and damage or harm can result.

When you're faced with cutting large stems, put aside your loppers and pick up a pruning saw instead.

Pruning Saws

When you find yourself straining to make a cut with those loppers, it's time to reach for your pruning saw. Depending on the model, most saws can make cuts up to 3 inches (7.5 cm) in diameter.

You might want to make your first pruning saw a folding saw that is easy to carry in a pocket. However, be sure that it has a way to be locked open when in use so it won't collapse on your hand. Wing nuts or spring mechanisms are common for this. Fixed-blade pruning saws are more expensive and more suitable for larger cuts.

Pruning saws are quite different from other types, so resist the temptation to use the saws from your wood shop for tree pruning. Most pruning-saw blades and handles are curved to help you get into the tight spaces of branch crotches and shrub bases. The teeth are most often sharpened to cut on the draw (when you are pulling). Some newer saws can cut on both the push and pull strokes; these are handy in tight spaces where you can't move the saw much. With practice, you will find that making a cut with a good pruning saw is almost effortless. Finally, most pruning-saw blades have teeth on only one side of the blade. Saws with teeth on both sides make it hard not to nick adjoining branches. Even with teeth on just one side, pruning saws can rub the bark from nearby branches, so use care.

Chain Saws

Chain saws come in many makes, models, and sizes. They are useful for making cuts of 3 inches (7.5 cm)

For delicate pruning jobs, like trimming clematis vines or deadheading flowers, hand-held bypass pruners are best.

and larger in diameter, depending on the size and power of the saw. Used improperly, chain saws can cause serious personal injury, so make sure you follow the safety procedures outlined in the owner's manual. For home pruning, only use your chain saw when you are standing on the ground, and always keep it below shoulder level. Leave the climbing to a trained arborist.

Pole Pruners and Saws

Pole pruners can have either wood or fiberglass shafts. The cutting part may be bypass pruners, which are operated with a rope, or a stationary saw blade. Pole pruners are very handy for making overhead cuts and are preferable to using ladders. As a general rule, if you can't reach a branch with your regular tools or with pole pruners, consider getting an arborist on the job.

Loppers are best for stems up to 1³/₄ inches (4.3 cm) in diameter. The long handles make pruning thorny stems easier!

A sharp, sturdy, hand-held pruning saw is a necessity for cutting larger branches that you can reach from the ground.

Even if you can reach the branches with your saw or pruners, you still need to be careful when trimming overhead limbs. Only cut branches you can reach while standing well off to the side; don't assume that you'll be able to catch a falling branch before it hits you! Also, scout for hazards, like wasp or animal nests, before you decide to trim a limb yourself. For more safety tips, see "Pruning Tools and Power Lines."

Other Extension Tools

A variety of other extension pruning tools are available. Some are questionable in their usefulness or in their ability to make a clean cut. You may see, for instance, a tool that consists of a chain blade fixed in the middle of a rope. One end of the rope is thrown over a branch, and the chain is used to make large cuts that would normally be done with a pruning saw or chain saw. Because these chains don't enable you to make the three-step removal necessary for a large branch (see "Removing Larger Limbs" on page 58 for details), it is more likely that your cut with this tool will tear off a good deal of bark along with the limb. Likewise, electrical-powered extension chain saws don't allow you the control that you need to make a good cut—three step or otherwise—and damage is likely. For your own safety and the health of the tree, hire a qualified arborist for those big cuts that require climbing.

A few basic pruning tools are all you need to tackle most of your landscape plants; call a pro for heavy-duty work.

Pole pruners and saws are handy for making overhead cuts that you otherwise couldn't reach from the ground.

Hedge Shears

Hedge shears are best for non-selective heading cuts—the kinds of cuts you make when training a formal hedge. Hedge shears are appropriate only for the tender new shoot growth that was brought on by a previous shearing; don't try them for heavier cuts.

These tools can be powered manually or electrically. Manual shears that have one serrated blade and one straight blade are good for heavy-duty work. Electric trimmers can make a large job go more quickly, but they also make it easier to make mistakes more quickly. There's also the added hazard of cutting through the cord with a careless swipe of the shears. Gas-powered trimmers are heavy but powerful.

Knives

A sharp folding pocket knife, preferably with a slightly forward-curving blade, comes in handy for the quick removal of new watersprouts. It's also helpful for trimming other growth that might be a little too tough for rubbing off but not worth running for the hand pruners. Use the same standards with a knife as you would with other pruning tools: Leave no stubs and keep even the tiniest branch collars intact!

Machetes

Machetes are often used for shearing Christmas trees in commercial production and for shearing large masses of azaleas in the South soon after they bloom. They're not used too often in the home garden, but you may see them for sale. As with all pruning tools, they must be kept very sharp, and you should use them with great caution to avoid injury.

Tree paint has little or no benefit for protecting pruning wounds. A good cut is the best defense against disease.

When you use the right tools and the proper techniques, your landscape plants will be healthier and more beautiful.

Tree Paint

It was once thought that the application of tree paint to pruning wounds helped to promote healing and reduce decay. Modern research has proven that tree paint (also called wound dressing) has a neutral effect, at best. Making a proper pruning cut just outside the branch collar is the best way to help your tree recover from the wounds you inflict while pruning. So if you feel you must apply tree paint, save it for cosmetic use, when masking a big cut is desirable for aesthetic reasons.

Safety Equipment

Let's face it—pruning is definitely not one of the safest aspects of gardening. Twigs, sharp tools, and sometimes our own hurry to get things done can put us in danger. Make sturdy leather gloves and some kind of glasses a part of your standard safety gear for pruning. Many a leather glove has come between an experienced pruner and a nick from the shears; who would disagree that a sliced glove beats a trip to the emergency room for stitches any day? And most pruning jobs include some element of skinny, pointed twigs, sometimes moving unpredictably just outside your range of vision. For best protection consider wearing safety glasses, or at least your sunglasses or prescription glasses, when you head out to prune. See "Pruning Tools and Power Lines" for more safety tips.

Pruning Tools and Power Lines

When using pole pruners or any other extension tool, check carefully to make sure that there are no power lines running through or by the tree. Also remember that high-voltage electricity can arc over several feet (meters) outside the wires. Since you and your pole pruners do not want to be the ground for this electricity, stay far away from power lines. If tree limbs need to be pruned away from lines, call your electric company or a qualified arborist to do the work.

Safe pruning involves choosing the right tools; use a pole saw instead of a ladder and loppers for high cuts. Also avoid hazards like nests and power lines.

PRUNING SHRUBS AND HEDGES

Successful shrub and hedge pruning begins with careful plant selection. Ideally, you want a plant that can succeed in the growing conditions your garden has to offer. And you may want that same plant to perform some particular function in your garden, providing flowers, fruit, privacy, or some other purpose. Most important (as far as pruning is concerned), you want a plant that will fit in the amount of garden space you have available.

Chances are good that you have at least one problem shrub in your garden. Maybe that cute little shrub you bought in a moment of weakness at the garden center is now a giant, demanding frequent trimming to keep it out of the path to your door. Or perhaps you moved into a house with a carelessly planned (or unplanned) landscape, where the shrubs are tangled and fighting each other for room. Either way, a poor match between a plant, its growing conditions, and the demands placed on it can result in a lose-lose situation. You lose lots of precious gardening time pruning a poorly chosen plant, and the plant loses its natural character and grace as you try to control it.

A more successful (and low-maintenance) approach is to let the natural character of your shrub and hedge plants be your guide. Give flowering and fruiting shrubs plenty of space, so they can get the light and moisture they require. If you want a small or dense plant for a hedge or privacy screen, choose a compact or dwarf selection that will naturally need much less pruning. If you have a problem plant in your landscape, find out what the plant is and what its natural habits are; then you'll be able to decide if it's worth regular pruning or if it needs to be moved or replaced.

As you learn about your shrubs and hedges, you'll be working smarter: Your pruning chores will actually take less time, and they'll produce better, longer-lasting results. This chapter will guide you through the basics of effective shrub and hedge pruning. You'll also find handy tips on selecting easy-care plants. The "Guide to Shrubs and Hedges," starting on page 32, provides specific information on when and how to prune over 40 popular landscape plants.

Knowing when and how to prune effectively will help you get the best from your shrubs, whether you're growing them for their leaves, flowers, or showy fruits (like those of beautyberry [*Callicarpa* sp.]).

Shrub Pruning Basics

Much of the routine pruning you'll do around your yard involves trimming the shrubs to keep them tidy and vigorous. The techniques and timing will vary depending on whether the shrub is deciduous or evergreen.

Deciduous Shrubs

When pruning deciduous shrubs, take every opportunity to remove dead wood, always cutting back to a live bud or branch. Use thinning cuts to remove crossing, rubbing, or congested branches, following a schedule that uses flowering time as a guide. (See "Pruning Timetable for Deciduous Shrubs" for recommended pruning times.) Resist the temptation to shear a deciduous shrub with heading cuts, which encourage bushy growth on the branch tips, leaving the plant hollow and shaded in the center. Instead, thin back the longest branches; this will open the center to the light and encourage new growth and abundant flowering.

Many deciduous shrubs—including viburnums, forsythia, and beautyberries (*Callicarpa* spp.)—produce strong new stems when you periodically remove the old canes. Take out one-third of the oldest stems each year in late winter or early spring. With this kind of regular attention, the shrubs will bloom vigorously and never get out of control.

A similar technique works for shrubs with brightly colored stems, like red- or golden-twig dogwoods (such as *Cornus sericea* or *C. sericea* 'Flaviramea'). New stems tend to produce the best color, so in late winter each year, prune the oldest growth to just above the ground to keep the new growth coming.

Needle-leaved Evergreens

On needle-leaved evergreens, use thinning cuts during the summer to remove dead wood or branches that are getting out of bounds. Follow the branch back into the shrub to "hide" your cut, leaving a natural, feathered appearance. Shear only if you need a very formal look; otherwise, you'll ruin the plant's natural shape and

Snap off the spent flowers of rhododendrons to encourage future flowering.

Japanese pieris (*Pieris japonica*) seldom needs pruning; just trim off spent blooms and dead wood after flowering.

you'll have to keep shearing to maintain the shape you've imposed on it. Reserve heading cuts for encouraging a young plant to fill in, for pinching the "candles" of pines and firs, or for the rare severe pruning.

Very few needle-leaved evergreens can survive the kind of hard pruning that cuts back into wood with no needles, so rejuvenation is usually not an option. Yews (*Taxus* spp.) are an exception when the conditions are good; they happily regrow after being cut almost to the ground in midspring.

Broad-leaved Evergreens

Broad-leaved evergreens, including rhododendrons, mountain laurel (*Kalmia latifolia*), and Japanese aucuba (*Aucuba japonica*), need very little pruning. Use thinning cuts to remove dead, dying, crossing, or errant

Careful, planned pruning will help to guide the growth of your young shrubs, so they'll be well shaped at maturity.

Prune spring- and early-summer-blooming shrubs in late winter or early spring; trim later bloomers after flowering.

branches any time of the year that the wood is not frozen. Wait until just after flowering to make any heading cuts; deadhead rhododendrons at this time.

Healthy but overgrown broad-leaved evergreens will resprout if you cut them to within a foot (30 cm) of the ground, although it can take 2 to 4 years for plants to recover and look good again. If you need to rejuvenate a broad-leaved evergreen, wait until late winter to carry out this heavy pruning. To help the plant recover, keep the soil evenly moist, and add some compost and mulch to promote good root growth. Be patient—it may take several weeks for fresh shoots to emerge. Pinch the new stems as needed so the plant will fill in.

Some broad-leaved evergreens, such as heavenly bamboo (*Nandina domestica*), drooping leucothoe

Cutting stem tips back to a bud promotes branching; pruning back to a stem or the ground thins crowded growth.

Pruning Timetable for Deciduous Shrubs

Can't remember if you're supposed to prune your flowering shrubs before or after they bloom? Use these lists for easy reference.

During the Dormant Season

Abelia x *grandiflora* (glossy abelia)
Buddleia davidii (orange-eye butterfly bush)
Callicarpa spp. (beautyberries)
Caryopteris x *clandonensis* (bluebeard)
Hibiscus spp. (hibiscus)
Hydrangea spp. (most hydrangeas)
Lagerstroemia spp. (crape myrtles)
Nandina domestica (heavenly bamboo)
Rhus spp. (sumacs)
Spiraea spp. (summer-blooming spireas)
Vitex spp. (chaste trees)

Immediately after Flowering

Berberis spp. (barberry)
Buddleia alternifolia (fountain buddleia)
Chaenomeles spp. (flowering quince)
Clethra spp. (summersweets)
Cotinus spp. (smokebushes)
Cotoneaster spp. (cotoneasters)
Daphne spp. (daphnes)
Deutzia spp. (deutzias)
Euonymus spp. (euonymus)
Forsythia spp. (forsythias)
Hydrangea macrophylla (big-leaved hydrangea)
Kerria japonica (Japanese kerria)
Kalmia latifolia (mountain laurel)
Kolkwitzia amabilis (beautybush)
Ligustrum spp. (privets)
Lonicera spp. (shrubby honeysuckles)
Philadelphus spp. (mock oranges)
Pieris spp. (pieris)
Pyracantha spp. (pyracanthas)
Rhododendron spp. (rhododendrons and azaleas)
Spiraea spp. (spring-blooming spireas)
Syringa spp. (lilacs)
Viburnum spp. (viburnums)
Weigela spp. (weigelas)

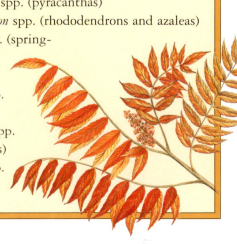

(*Leucothoe fontanesiana*), and mahonias (*Mahonia* spp.), grow in cane form. Thin them annually at the base, removing about one-third of the oldest growth.

A Pruning Problem-Solver

Proper pruning can go a long way toward keeping your shrubs healthy and looking good. But there are times when you may have a problem plant and wonder what to do with it. Pruning can't solve all the problems, but it may help with some of them.

Shrub Is Too Large If you need to dramatically reduce the size of a shrub quickly, cutting the whole thing to within 2 to 3 inches (5 to 7.5 cm) above the ground may be an option. (See "Shrubs That Survive Severe Pruning" for a list of shrubs that can tolerate this treatment.) Hard pruning to a basic aboveground framework works well for some shrubs that can't be cut to the ground; yews, boxwoods (*Buxus* spp.), and many of the broad-leaved evergreens respond nicely to this.

For a less-drastic solution, thin a few of the longest branches back to a main stem each year. Or consider removing the lower branches from the stems; some shrubs—like lilacs and panicle hydrangea (*Hydrangea paniculata*)—can make great little trees when pruned this way.

Whatever you do, don't just shear all the stems back to the same level. New stems will simply regrow from the heading cuts, and you'll be back where you started in as little as a year or two.

Prune camellias (*Camellia* spp.) in late winter or early spring to thin out the center of the plant.

Shrub Is Loose and Leggy First be sure that your sprawling or leggy shrub has all of the light that it needs. Open growth often results when a light-starved plant is reaching, and pruning won't correct this. If lack of light isn't the problem, pinch out young stem tips or use selective heading cuts on older stems to encourage bud growth.

Stems Are Crowded and Tangled Use thinning cuts to open the center of the plant to light and air. Be sure to do this gradually, over a period of several seasons, as that inner growth may need some time to adjust to higher light levels.

Shrub Has Few or No Flowers Thinning out the oldest stems, especially on mature plants, will allow

Unlike most hydrangeas, big-leaved hydrangea (*Hydrangea macrophylla*) blooms on the previous year's stems.

Shrubs That Survive Severe Pruning

It may seem like a drastic step, but cutting some shrubs to within 2 to 3 inches (5 to 7.5 cm) of the ground in late winter is a great way to reduce plant size and promote better flowering. Below is a list of plants that can take this sort of treatment.

Abelia x *grandiflora* (glossy abelia)
Buddleia davidii (orange-eye butterfly bush)
Forsythia spp. (forsythias)
Hibiscus spp. (hibiscus)
Hydrangea quercifolia (oak-leaved hydrangea)
Ligustrum spp. (privets)
Spiraea spp. (spireas)
Syringa spp. (lilacs)

A combination of careful plant selection and annual pruning will help your shrub plantings stay bushy and beautiful.

better light penetration and encourage vigorous new blooming wood. Also, make sure you prune shrubs that bloom on last year's wood—such as weigelas and lilacs—as soon as they are finished blooming. If you wait too long, you'll cut off the flower buds that have formed for next year's bloom.

Sheared-shrub Renovation

What about that forsythia or viburnum that was shorn endlessly by the previous property owner? With proper pruning and some patience, you can restore the shrub to its natural form and character.

Some shrubs (including those listed in "Shrubs That Survive Severe Pruning") will regrow better than ever if you cut all the old stems to just above the ground. Thin and trim the new growth as needed to match the plant's natural shape.

Other shrubs respond better to thinning cuts that open the center of the plant to light and air. Gradually thin out some of the oldest stems each year. Prune and train the new growth as needed.

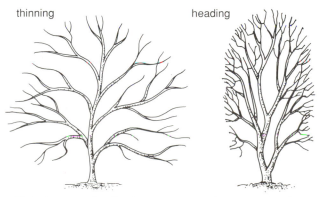

Thinning—cutting back to a stem or the ground—gives a natural feel; heading can make a plant look awkward.

Pruning back some of the longest stems each year will gradually help to reduce the size of an overgrown shrub.

For full growth, shape formal hedges so the top is narrower than the base to get even exposure to sunlight.

Pruning and Training Hedges

Hedges can be short or tall, narrow or wide, formal or informal. The size and style of your hedge will depend on the plants you have chosen or inherited, their natural growth habit, and your method of managing them.

Newly Planted Hedges

If you plant your new hedge from bareroot stock, cut the top of each plant back by about half. This will give the roots a chance to get established before the demands of top growth are placed on them, and you will get a fuller, more functional hedge more quickly.

Container-grown or balled-and-burlapped nursery stock will need little pruning at planting time. Just remove any dead wood that you notice.

A common and understandable mistake is allowing hedge plants to grow to their desired height before the first trimming or shearing. This approach results in a hedge with long, weak inner growth that only branches toward the tips. This is particularly a problem with formal hedges, since the inner growth may be unable to support the weight of the headed-back top. Strong winds or heavy rain or snow may cause weak branches to split off, leaving ugly gaps in the hedge.

A better approach is to begin pinching very young growth soon after planting to encourage it to fill in. Regular pinching will give the plants in an informal hedge a full, balanced look. If you decide to invest the time in maintaining a formal hedge, start shearing the plants as soon as they begin to grow noticeably, even if you want the mature hedge to be tall. It will take longer to get the full effect, but the strong, dense growth will be able to support its own weight and a significant snow load, too.

Established Formal Hedges

Treat established formal hedges as you would a lawn, trimming or shearing as needed through the growing season. As with grass, the best strategy is to cut little but often. Frequent heading cuts encourage buds to break behind the cuts, promoting dense growth that

> ## Plants for Informal Hedges
>
> Many of the hedge plants listed here are easy to manage with the annual removal of the oldest stems at ground level or—in the case of hemlock—with no pruning at all.
> *Abelia* x *grandiflora* (glossy abelia)
> *Forsythia* x *intermedia* (showy border forsythia)
> *Ligustrum obtusifolium* var. *regelianum* (Regel border privet)
> *Rosa* spp. (shrub roses)
> *Tsuga canadensis* (Canada hemlock)
> *Viburnum* spp. (viburnums)

A stake-and-string guide is handy to direct your cuts; this is critical for good results on formal hedges.

fills in gaps. Remove only a small bit of growth at a time, never cutting into hardened-off wood. On needle-leaved evergreen hedges, such as yews, shear when dew is on the plants; this can help reduce browning on the newly cut tips. Stop shearing all hedges before late summer, so the new growth coming in can harden before the first freezing weather.

If your hedge has a well-defined shape, you can probably get away with shearing by eye. If a perfect line is critical, or if you are shaping a young formal hedge, you may want to set up post-and-string guides to direct your cuts. Always shape a formal hedge so that it is narrower at the top than at the bottom. This enables sunlight to reach the lower branches, making your hedge full to the ground. Hedges that are wider at the top tend to have "bare ankles" and over time become progressively naked from the bottom up. If this happens, consider rejuvenating and reshaping the hedge.

Established Informal Hedges

Prune an informal flowering hedge as you would if the same plants were growing individually. Use thinning cuts to keep the plants actively growing and blooming. Where the sides of two plants meet, allow the branches to mingle a bit so the plants "mesh" together. Save heading cuts for directing stray branches or trimming

Hedge shears work fine for light trimming, but for extensive work, electric or gas-powered shears may be more practical.

> ## Hedge Plants for Minimal Pruning
>
> The hedge plants listed here tend to stay compact and within a limited size range. You may decide to clip them occasionally if you want a more regular look.
>
> *Acanthopanax sieboldianus* (five-leaved aralia)
> *Buxus microphylla* var. *koreana* (Korean boxwood)
> *Euonymus alata* 'Compacta' (dwarf burning bush)
> *Taxus cuspidata* 'Capitata' (pyramidal Japanese yew)
> *Thuja occidentalis* 'Emerald' or 'Holmstrup' (American arborvitae cultivars)

out unwanted wood; avoid shearing altogether. If renewal is necessary, determine if your hedge plants can tolerate being cut to or near the ground; as they regrow, train them as if they were young plants in a new hedge. (Look up your plant in the "Guide to Shrubs and Hedges," starting on page 32, or check out "Shrub Pruning Basics" on page 26 to see if your shrubs can take this kind of treatment.)

Overgrown-hedge Renovation

Many overgrown hedges will respond well to severe pruning. Plants that quickly regrow when rejuvenated include privets (*Ligustrum* spp.), ninebark (*Physocarpus opulifolius*), pyracanthas (*Pyracantha* spp.), barberries (*Berberis* spp.), bayberries (*Myrica* spp.), spireas (*Spiraea* spp.), forsythias (*Forsythia* spp.), and buckthorns (*Rhamnus* spp.). A few of the evergreens can also be renewed in this way, including boxwoods (*Buxus* spp.), hollies (*Ilex* spp.), and yews (*Taxus* spp.). The other needle-leaved evergreens cannot regrow from bare wood, so don't try this on spruces, pines, firs, or hemlocks.

One approach is to rejuvenate the hedge by pruning the stems almost to the ground or by cutting them back hard to a basic framework within a foot or two (30 to 60 cm) of the ground. It looks quite drastic, but never fear—new growth will appear in a few weeks. After a year, you'll have a dense, bushy, more manageable hedge that you can begin to shape and train as you wish.

If you'd prefer not to lose the screening effect of a shrubby deciduous hedge entirely, you can rejuvenate it more gradually. Prune one-third of the oldest stems each year, as you would for a stand-alone shrub; after 3 years, all the growth will be fresh and easy to train. This technique will also allow you to convert a high-maintenance formal hedge into an easy-care informal one. The hedge won't look great during the transition, but it will still serve the purpose.

Abelia x *grandiflora*   Caprifoliaceae

GLOSSY ABELIA

Glossy abelia is an easy-care shrub that produces pink or white flowers from spring through summer. Prune out some of the oldest stems each spring to encourage vigorous new shoots.

DESCRIPTION: Glossy abelia has a rounded habit, with loosely arching purplish red branches. It grows 4–6 feet (1.2–1.8 m) tall. Pale pink or white flowers appear in late spring, then sporadically until frost. The glossy green leaves often turn bronze or burgundy when cool weather arrives. Semi-evergreen in most climates, it may drop its leaves during very cold winters. Performs best in well-drained soil in full sun or partial shade. Zones 5–8.

WHEN TO PRUNE: In late winter or early spring before growth begins.

HOW TO PRUNE: Prune out any winter-damaged branches. Glossy abelia flowers on the current season's shoots; encourage vigorous new growth by cutting about one-third of the oldest remaining branches to the ground. Don't shear or leave stubs. Rejuvenate overgrown plants by cutting the entire shrub back to the ground.

SPECIAL TIPS: In Zone 5, glossy abelia will likely need heavy spring pruning to remove winter-damaged growth. As a result, the plant seldom reaches full size there. For compact growth in warmer areas, try the low-growing 'Prostrata' or the semidwarf 'Sherwoodii'.

Berberis spp. Berberidaceae	*Buddleia* spp. Loganiaceae

BARBERRIES

BUTTERFLY BUSHES

Barberries have thorny stems that make them particularly useful for hedges and barriers. Prune a few of the oldest stems to ground level in winter or spring to thin crowded growth.

Orange-eye butterfly bush blooms on new wood, so heavy annual pruning will promote more flowers. Cut out one-third of the oldest stems, or prune all of them to 8 inches (20 cm).

DESCRIPTION: Barberries produce small yellow flowers in spring, followed by berries in summer and fall. Leaves are deciduous, evergreen, or semi-evergreen. Sharp thorns not only make barberries excellent for barriers but also make them hard to prune and cause them to trap leaf litter and rubbish. They prefer full sun and good drainage.

B. julianae (wintergreen barberry): Has blue-black berries and shiny evergreen leaves that may turn bright red during a cold winter. Height 3–6 feet (90–180 cm). Zones 6–8.

B. thunbergii (Japanese barberry): Has a spreading habit. Deciduous leaves are green in spring and summer; they turn red before dropping in fall to reveal red berries. Height 4–6 feet (1.2–1.8 m). Zones 4–8.

WHEN TO PRUNE: In winter or spring after flowering.

HOW TO PRUNE: Wear leather gloves and long sleeves to protect yourself from the thorns. Remove a few shoots at ground level each year to thin out the stems and invigorate the plant. Resist the temptation to shear; barberries look great as informal hedges.

SPECIAL TIPS: *B. thunbergii* var. *atropurpurea* 'Crimson Pygmy' is a popular purple-leaved cultivar that is naturally low-growing, giving a compact effect without regular pruning.

DESCRIPTION: These delightful butterfly magnets produce copious fragrant flowers in summer. The silvery gray foliage is deciduous. Plants prefer full sun and fertile, loamy soil.

B. alternifolia (fountain buddleia): Has arching branches; height to 12 feet (3.6 m). Its lavender-colored flowers bloom in the leaf joints of the previous year's growth. Zones 4–8.

B. davidii (orange-eye butterfly bush): Grows upright at first; develops an arching habit with age. Height 5–8 feet (1.5–2.4 m). Purple flowers bloom on the current season's growth. Its cultivars may have white, red, pink, or violet-blue flowers. Zones 6–8. Plants often die back to the ground each winter in the northern part of this range, but new shoots generally appear from the roots.

WHEN TO PRUNE: Prune fountain buddleia in summer after it blooms, before the flower buds form for the following year. Prune orange-eye butterfly bush in late winter or early spring before growth begins.

HOW TO PRUNE: Each year, cut one-third of the oldest stems to within 8 inches (20 cm) of the ground. To rejuvenate overgrown plants, cut all the stems to this height.

SPECIAL TIPS: Annual pruning keeps these plants growing and blooming vigorously.

Buxus spp.   Buxaceae   *Callicarpa* spp.   Verbenaceae

BOXWOODS   # BEAUTYBERRIES

*Boxwoods generally don't need much pruning to look good;
simply trim out winter damage and stray branches as needed.
Overgrown plants respond well to heavy pruning.*

*Keep beautyberries vigorous and productive by removing one-
third of the oldest stems in late winter or early spring. Rejuvenate neglected plants by cutting them to just above the ground.*

DESCRIPTION: Boxwoods bear glossy evergreen leaves
in pairs on slender branches. They're grown most
often for their foliage effect as hedges, barriers, and
foundation plants; the spring flowers are inconspicuous. Many cultivars are available, varying in
height, habit, and hardiness.

B. microphylla (little-leaved boxwood): Compact,
dense, rounded shrub; height to 3 feet (90 cm).
Zones 6–8.

B. sempervirens (common boxwood): May grow as
a shrub or small tree; height to 15 feet (4.5 m). The
leaves may bronze in winter. Zones 6–8.

WHEN TO PRUNE: In late spring after the first flush of
growth.

HOW TO PRUNE: Routine pruning simply involves
cutting out any winter-damaged or awkward-
looking branches. Rejuvenate overgrown or winter-
damaged plants by pruning heavily—almost to
the ground. For a formal hedge, trim periodically
throughout the growing season. Stop pruning by
midsummer, so the new growth has plenty of time
to harden off before cold weather arrives.

SPECIAL TIPS: Boxwoods are prone to winter damage
(browned leaves and dead stem tips) in cold-winter
areas. To minimize damage, plant young boxwoods
in a sheltered location; protect exposed, established ones from strong wind and winter sun with
burlap screens.

DESCRIPTION: Beautyberries are deciduous shrubs
admired for their brightly colored clusters of
berries in fall. They require full sun and well-
drained soil that is evenly moist.

C. americana (American beautyberry or French
mulberry): Loose, open shrub; height to 8 feet
(2.4 m). Lavender-pink flowers appear in summer
on the current season's growth, followed by violet
to magenta fruits. Zones 7–10.

C. japonica (Japanese beautyberry): Has an arching
habit; height 4–8 feet (1.2–2.4 m). Pink or white
summer flowers are followed by clusters of bright
purple berries that persist into winter. Zones 5–8.

WHEN TO PRUNE: In late winter to early spring.

HOW TO PRUNE: Cut one-third of the oldest or
weakest branches to the ground each year. To
rejuvenate an overgrown beautyberry, cut the
entire shrub back to a few inches above the ground.

SPECIAL TIPS: As with other summer bloomers, annual
pruning encourages vigorous blooming and fruiting and helps to keep the plant a manageable size.

Camellia spp. Theaceae

CAMELLIAS

Thinning crowded stems after flowering will keep camellias open to light and air, reducing the development of diseases and encouraging more blooms next year.

DESCRIPTION: Camellias are evergreen shrubs or trees that perform best in light to medium shade—the high shade of tall pines is said to be best. They grow 4–15 feet (1.2–4.5 m) tall, depending on the climate and cultivar. For best results, provide well-drained, humus-rich soil and a sheltered spot protected from wind.

C. japonica (common camellia): Upright tree, pyramidal or oval in form, with one or many trunks. Blooms begin to open in late fall. Depending on the cultivar, the single or double flowers can be pink, red, or white; some have showy stamens or streaked petals. Zones 7–9.

C. sasanqua (sasanqua camellia): Has a more open and shrubby form; height 4–6 feet (1.2–1.8 m) or more. The white or pink flowers, single or double, bloom in fall. Zones 7–9.

WHEN TO PRUNE: In winter or early spring after the plant finishes blooming.

HOW TO PRUNE: Remove crossing or rubbing limbs. Thin the remaining stems to open the plant to sunlight and air; this will improve flowering and help to prevent fungal diseases. Remove spent flowers.

SPECIAL TIPS: Clean up dropped blooms and pick any spent flowers off the plant to reduce overwintering sites for fungal diseases.

Carpinus betulus Betulaceae

EUROPEAN HORNBEAM

European hornbeam makes a sturdy, attractive hedge. It grows relatively slowly, so it doesn't need frequent pruning to stay in good shape.

DESCRIPTION: European hornbeam is a deciduous tree that grows in a dense, upright oval form. It can reach 50 feet (15 m) if unpruned; trimming it as a hedge will control the size. Hornbeam prefers full sun and well-drained soil. Zones 5–7.

WHEN TO PRUNE: Prune hornbeam hedges in late winter and through the growing season as needed.

HOW TO PRUNE: Because of its compact growth and regular form, European hornbeam is well adapted for use as screens or hedges. Trim established hornbeam hedges once during the dormant season and as needed in spring and summer to keep the shape. Be sure to make the last trimming by midsummer, which will give any new growth an opportunity to harden off before the first freeze.

SPECIAL TIPS: If you have a neglected hornbeam hedge or one that has overgrown its space, you can reclaim it with hard pruning. Trim one side back to the main stems one winter; cut back the other side the following year. See the Hornbeams entry on page 65 to find out how to prune these plants as trees.

Chaenomeles speciosa   Rosaceae

FLOWERING QUINCE

Pruning out a few of the oldest, most crowded stems after blooming will keep flowering quince vigorous and promote more blooms next spring. Wear gloves to avoid the thorns!

DESCRIPTION: Flowering quince is a thorny, deciduous, spreading shrub. It grows in a mounded form 4–8 feet (1.2–2.4 m) tall. Showy single or double flowers in white or shades of red or pink appear in early spring. Lumpy yellow 2-inch (5 cm) fruits form in fall; like persimmons, they're edible but astringent when unripe. Flowering quince grows best in full sun and soil with perfect drainage. Zones 4–8.

WHEN TO PRUNE: In late spring, after flowering.

HOW TO PRUNE: Don heavy leather gloves and long sleeves to defend yourself from the stout thorns on this plant. Selectively remove branches to open the shrub to sunlight. Rejuvenate an old, overgrown, poorly blooming plant by cutting it to a few inches above the ground.

SPECIAL TIPS: Much like barberries, flowering quince tends to trap litter—natural leaf litter and the other kind—with its thorns and twiggy growth. Keeping the shrub thinned and open as described above serves two purposes: It keeps the plant blooming vigorously, and it allows for good air flow through the plant. That way, the litter will blow through and not mat in the stems, where you will eventually have to fish it out.

Cornus sericea   Cornaceae

RED-OSIER DOGWOOD

The colorful stems of red-osier dogwood add excitement to a dull winter landscape. Prune out one-third of the oldest stems in late winter or after flowering to encourage new growth.

DESCRIPTION: The red stems of this deciduous shrub look dramatic against the winter snow. It forms a loose, broadly rounded outline to 7 feet (2.1 m) tall. Flat-topped clusters of white flowers appear in spring, followed by white berries that contrast nicely with the reddish fall foliage. Red-osier dogwood prefers moist, humus-rich soil; its native habitat includes swampy sites. Zones 2–7.

WHEN TO PRUNE: In late winter (before growth begins) or after flowering.

HOW TO PRUNE: Cut one-third of the oldest stems to the ground each year. To rejuvenate an old, overgrown, or spindly plant, cut all stems to a few inches above the ground.

SPECIAL TIPS: Annual pruning keeps this plant growing vigorously and producing the desirable red stems.

COTONEASTERS

Cotoneasters have a naturally tidy growth habit that seldom calls for pruning. Simply trim out dead, damaged, or poorly placed branches as you spot them.

DESCRIPTION: Cotoneasters can be evergreen, semi-evergreen, or deciduous, depending on the species and climate. They bear pink or white flowers in spring, followed by reddish fruits in fall. Cotoneasters require full sun and good drainage.
C. apiculatus (cranberry cotoneaster): Deciduous. Grows to 20 inches (50 cm). Zones 5–7.
C. divaricatus (spreading cotoneaster): Deciduous. Height to 5 feet (1.5 m); often more wide than tall. Distinguished by purplish stems and excellent red fall foliage. Zones 5–8.
C. horizontalis (rockspray cotoneaster): Deciduous. Has a spreading, mounding, layered habit; height to 3 feet (90 cm). Zones 5–8.
C. salicifolius (willowleaf cotoneaster): Evergreen or semi-evergreen. Has an arching form and slender, glossy leaves; height to 12 feet (3.6 m). Zones 6–8.

WHEN TO PRUNE: Anytime, although late spring is best if you enjoy seeing the flowers.

HOW TO PRUNE: Rarely needs pruning. Cut dead, crossing, or awkwardly placed branches back to a healthy main stem or down to ground level.

SPECIAL TIPS: Plants are prone to fire blight, a bacterial disease that causes leaves and shoots to turn black. If you see these symptoms, cut out the affected parts with at least 6 inches (15 cm) of healthy wood. Dip or wipe pruners with isopropyl alcohol between cuts to avoid spreading the disease.

HAWTHORNS

With regular pruning, hawthorns can grow into sturdy, attractive hedges. Enjoy their white spring flowers, glossy summer leaves, bright fall color, and showy winter fruits.

DESCRIPTION: Hawthorns are thorny, deciduous large shrubs or small trees with single or multiple trunks. White flowers appear in midspring and are followed by reddish fruits in the fall and—in a good year—remarkable fall color. They can withstand heavy pruning for hedge use. They require full sun and good drainage.
C. crus-galli (cockspur hawthorn): Has a horizontally layered outline and purplish bronze fall color; height to 30 feet (9 m) if left untrimmed. The cultivar 'Inermis' doesn't have thorns. Zones 4–7.
C. phaenopyrum (Washington hawthorn): Height to 25 feet (7.5 m) if left untrimmed. Fall color can be orange, purple, or scarlet. Zones 4–8.
C. viridis (green hawthorn): Height to 25 feet (7.5 m) if left untrimmed; fall colors in purples and reds. The cultivar 'Winter King' is well known for its bright, persistent red berries. Zones 4–7.

WHEN TO PRUNE: In late winter and during the growing season as needed.

HOW TO PRUNE: Young hawthorn hedges need regular trimming to encourage dense, bushy growth. Trim or shear established hedges as needed to keep their shape. Stop pruning by midsummer so any new growth can harden off before cold weather arrives.

SPECIAL TIPS: See the Hawthorns entry on page 68 to learn how to prune these plants as trees.

Daphne spp.   Thymelaceae

DAPHNES

Daphnes will cover themselves in fragrant spring flowers year after year with little or no pruning. Simply trim out any damaged or poorly placed shoots after flowering.

DESCRIPTION: Daphnes are primarily grown for their early fragrant flowers. They prefer partial shade and perfectly drained, gravelly or sandy soil that doesn't dry out; mulch will help to keep the roots evenly moist.

   D. x *burkwoodii* (Burkwood daphne): Spreading shrub; height 2–5 feet (60–150 cm). Its blue-green leaves are evergreen in the South and deciduous in the North. Pink buds open to creamy white fragrant flowers in early spring. 'Carol Mackie' is a popular variegated cultivar. Zones 4–7.

   D. odora (winter daphne): Also has a low, spreading habit; height 2–5 feet (60–150 cm). Bears glossy, evergreen foliage and fragrant, rosy purple flowers that appear in late winter. Zones 6–8.

WHEN TO PRUNE: In spring after flowering.

HOW TO PRUNE: Daphnes usually need minimal pruning. Cut out winter-damaged stems and awkwardly placed shoots.

Deutzia spp.   Saxifragaceae

DEUTZIAS

Prune deutzias as soon as possible after they bloom in spring. Thin out a few of the oldest stems each year to keep plants vigorous and free-blooming.

DESCRIPTION: Deutzias are deciduous, spring-blooming shrubs that prefer well-drained, evenly moist soil and full sun.

   D. gracilis (slender deutzia): Has a broad, mounding habit with arching branches and lance-shaped leaves; height 2–5 feet (60–150 cm). White flowers appear in late spring. Zones 5–8.

   D. x *lemoinei* (lemoine deutzia): A hybrid that grows 5–7 feet (1.5–2.1 m); known for its particularly showy white flowers. Zones 4–8.

   D. scabra (fuzzy deutzia): Has an upright, fountain-like form; height 5–8 feet (1.5–2.4 m). The green leaves are fuzzy with tufts of hair. White or pink flower clusters open in late spring or early summer. Zones 6–8.

WHEN TO PRUNE: In summer, immediately after flowering. If you wait until fall or spring, you'll cut off the flower buds and your plants won't bloom the next season.

HOW TO PRUNE: Thin out crowded plants by cutting a few of the weakest, oldest stems to the ground each year.

EUONYMUS

BEECHES

Burning bush is popular as a specimen shrub and an informal hedge. Allow ample room for each plant to develop, and it will need only minimal pruning to keep its shape.

A beech hedge is a dramatic addition to any large property. Several trimmings, starting when the hedge is small, will promote dense growth and a smooth, formal look.

DESCRIPTION: Euonymus are deciduous or evergreen shrubs or small trees that thrive in moist, humus-rich, well-drained soil. They are great for informal hedges. Deciduous species grow best in full sun; evergreens prefer a shaded spot protected from strong sun and wind.

    E. alata (burning bush): Deciduous shrub with an upright, rounded habit; height 12–15 feet (3.6–4.5 m). With age, thin "wings" of bark form on the branches. Fall foliage turns brilliant red, fading to pink; leaves drop to reveal pink-and-red seed capsules. Zones 4–8.

    E. kiautschovica (spreading euonymus): Semi-evergreen; height 8–10 feet (2.1–3 m). Inconspicuous flowers bloom in summer, followed by reddish seed capsules in fall. Severe winters can burn (brown) the foliage badly. Zones 5–8.

WHEN TO PRUNE: Prune during the dormant months; during very cold winters, wait until late spring.

HOW TO PRUNE: Although they withstand heavy pruning, euonymus rarely need pruning when they have the room they require. Trim burning bush as needed to keep its shape. If spreading euonymus is winter-burned, wait to prune out the damage until all of it is revealed—generally by late spring.

SPECIAL TIPS: *E. alata* 'Compacta' is a slow-growing form that may be more suitable for smaller residential properties than the species.

DESCRIPTION: Beeches are deciduous trees that make impressive hedges for large properties. Their leaves tend to persist through the winter with a golden-bronze fall color that pales a bit after every rain; by spring, the leaves are positively ghostly. Beeches prosper in full sun and well-drained, moist soil. They are extremely sensitive to soil compaction and other kinds of root disturbance.

    F. grandifolia (American beech): Height 50–70 feet (15–21 m) when left untrimmed. Leaves open silvery green and turn dark green as they age. Zones 4–8.

    F. sylvatica (European beech): Similar to American beech in appearance and landscape value; leaves may be slightly smaller. Zones 5–7.

WHEN TO PRUNE: Trim beech hedges as needed through the growing season; stop by midsummer to give the new growth a chance to harden off before cold weather.

HOW TO PRUNE: For a formal hedge, clip as needed from the time the trees are planted.

SPECIAL TIPS: Bear in mind that the wood of beech is very strong and dense—like nothing else to which you've ever put hedge trimmers. Tools that are not up to the task will tear the wood rather than make clean cuts, making your job harder and injuring the plants. See the Beeches entry on page 69 for tips on pruning them in classic shade-tree form.

Forsythia x *intermedia*   Oleaceae

SHOWY BORDER FORSYTHIA

Prune forsythias after flowering to avoid removing next spring's buds. Remove one-third of the oldest stems each year, or reclaim overgrown plants by cutting all stems to just above the ground.

DESCRIPTION: This deciduous shrub has an arching habit. It can grow to 8 feet (2.4 m) tall if left untrimmed. Bright yellow flowers generally appear in early spring before the leaves. Flower buds may be killed off during a severe winter, in which case plants will skip blooming for that year. Fall color can be a nice yellow-purple. Zones 4–8.

WHEN TO PRUNE: In late spring, just after flowering. Summer, fall, or late winter pruning will remove the flower buds, reducing or eliminating the next spring's show.

HOW TO PRUNE: Cut one-third of the oldest stems to the ground each year to encourage the production of vigorous new stems. To rejuvenate overgrown or poorly shaped plants, cut all the stems to a few inches above the ground.

SPECIAL TIPS: A walk through a suburban neighborhood in midspring will often reveal some of the worst pruning mistakes people make. Forsythias that have few or no flowers were probably pruned too late the previous season. Plants pruned into cubes or globes look stiff and awkward; ones that have never been trimmed are a tangled mess. Keep your plants growing and flowering vigorously by respecting their natural arching habit. Prune off whole stems to the ground, not just the tips; use hand pruners or loppers, not hedge shears!

Hibiscus spp.   Malvaceae

MALLOW

Mallows produce their colorful summer blooms on new stems. In late winter or early spring, trim one-third of the stems back to the ground to encourage new flowering growth.

DESCRIPTION: Mallows are woody perennials, shrubs, and small trees grown for their showy summer flowers. Both of the species described here thrive in full sun and in soil with steady moisture.

H. coccineus (scarlet rose mallow): Bears 5–6-inch (12–15 cm) bright red flowers throughout the summer. Height 6–12 feet (1.8–3.6 m). Native to coastal swamps, it thrives in imperfectly drained soil. Grows as a multistemmed shrub in Zone 9 and a woody perennial in Zones 5–8.

H. syriacus (rose-of-Sharon): Shrub or small tree; height to 12 feet (3.6 m). Bears 3–5-inch (7.5–12 cm) blooms in white, red, pink, or violet throughout the summer. Doesn't tolerate very wet or very dry soil. Zones 5–8.

WHEN TO PRUNE: In late winter or early spring, before growth begins.

HOW TO PRUNE: Cut one-third of the oldest stems to the ground each year. Scarlet rose mallow stems may die to the ground each winter; remove these before new shoots emerge from the crown.

SPECIAL TIPS: Summer bloomers like these hibiscus bloom best when growing vigorously; annual pruning encourages this.

HYDRANGEAS

Unlike many other hydrangeas, big–leaved hydrangea (Hydrangea macrophylla) blooms on the previous season's wood. Prune this species just after flowering.

DESCRIPTION: Hydrangeas are deciduous, spring- or summer-blooming shrubs. They thrive in partial shade to full sun and in evenly moist, humus-rich soil with good drainage.

H. arborescens (hills-of-snow): Forms a 2–5 foot (60–150 cm) spreading mound. Flat or rounded flower clusters bloom on the current season's wood from spring into summer. Zones 4–8.

H. macrophylla (big-leaved hydrangea): Bears pink or blue flowers on previous year's wood. Zones 6–8.

H. paniculata (panicle hydrangea): Height to 15 feet (4.5 m) when trained as a tree; can also grow as a multistemmed shrub. Pyramidal clusters of creamy white flowers bloom on the current season's wood in summer. The cultivar 'Grandiflora' is the popular peegee hydrangea. Zones 4–9.

H. quercifolia (oak-leaved hydrangea): Has a more open form than the other shrub hydrangeas; height to 6 feet (1.8 m). Cinnamon brown bark peels off in layers; the 10-inch (25 cm) pyramidal flower clusters change from white to pink to brown. Zones 5–8.

WHEN TO PRUNE: Prune big-leaved hydrangeas in summer after they bloom. Trim others in late winter or early spring, before growth begins.

HOW TO PRUNE: Cut one-third of the oldest growth on shrub hydrangeas to the ground each year. To rejuvenate overgrown shrubs, cut all of the stems to a few inches above the ground.

HOLLIES

Female plants of winterberry (Ilex verticillata) produce loads of showy red fruits with a little late-winter pruning. Plant both males and females to get berries.

DESCRIPTION: Hollies can be evergreen or deciduous shrubs or trees. They prefer full sun or partial shade, a location out of the wind, and moist, well-drained, humus-rich soil. Some of the shrubby species are covered below; for information on growing tree-type hollies, see the Hollies entry on page 71.

I. crenata (Japanese holly): Densely layered, compact evergreen with small leaves and black berries. The species grows to a height of 15 feet (4.5 m); cultivars tend to be more compact. Zones 6–8.

I. glabra (inkberry): Bears shiny, medium green, evergreen leaves and black berries. Although the species approaches 10 feet (3 m), cultivars such as 'Compacta' are smaller. Zones 5–9.

I. x meserveae (blue holly): Spiny evergreen with blue-green leaves, purplish stems, and red berries. Height to 7 feet (2.1 m). Zones 5–7.

I. verticillata (winterberry): Has a twiggy, rounded habit; height 6–10 feet (1.8–3 m). It loses its leaves in fall, revealing clusters of bright red berries. Thrives in poorly drained soil. Zones 4–9.

WHEN TO PRUNE: Prune Japanese holly, inkberry, and blue holly in late spring or early summer after the new growth has hardened off. Prune winterberry in late winter.

HOW TO PRUNE: Prune the evergreens to shape as needed. To prune winterberry, cut one-third of the oldest stems to ground level.

Juniperus spp.   Cupressaceae   *Kalmia latifolia*   Ericaceae

JUNIPERS   # MOUNTAIN LAUREL

Junipers tend to have naturally attractive growth habits and seldom need pruning. Trim stray stems back to where they join another branch or to the ground.

Low-maintenance mountain laurel needs little or no pruning to keep its dramatic, twisting form. Thin out stray branches after flowering. Remove spent blooms, if desired.

DESCRIPTION: Junipers are evergreen shrubs or trees. Their scale- or needle-like foliage comes in shades of green, blue, and yellow. The branches are adorned with bluish or greenish berry-like cones.

J. chinensis (Chinese juniper): Available in both tree and shrub forms. The shrub forms are frequently mounded or layered in habit and have blue or gray-green foliage; height 4–6 feet (1.2–1.8 m). Tree forms grow to 50 feet (15 m). Zones 4–8.

J. horizontalis (creeping juniper): Has a ground-hugging habit; height less than 1 foot (30 cm) in most cases. Many cultivars available. Zones 2–8.

J. sabina (savin juniper): Has an upright, vase-shaped form; height to 6 feet (1.8 m). Lower-growing cultivars reach 18–24 inches (45–60 cm) and are mounded or layered. Zones 3–8.

WHEN TO PRUNE: During the dormant season or as needed through the summer.

HOW TO PRUNE: To retain the natural character of the plant, remove individual branches where they join another branch union or at the ground. Avoid shearing or leaving stubs.

SPECIAL TIPS: Phomopsis blight sometimes kills young shoots, especially in spring and during wet weather. If blight is a problem, prune off affected branches and destroy them. Sanitize pruners between cuts by dipping or wiping with isopropyl alcohol.

DESCRIPTION: This picturesque native is rounded when young, often developing into an irregular form that exposes a bare, ropy trunk. It can grow to 15 feet (4.5 m) tall. It has dark green, glossy evergreen leaves and, in late spring, showy clusters of whitish flowers, banded in shades of pink. Mountain laurel grows well in evenly moist, well-drained, acid soil, with light shade and protection from wind and winter sun. Zones 4–7.

WHEN TO PRUNE: In summer after flowering.

HOW TO PRUNE: Remove spent flowers to promote flowering for the following year. If necessary, remove the occasional stray branch back to the ground or to another branch; don't leave stubs. If the growing conditions are favorable, overgrown mountain laurel may respond to hard rejuvenation pruning; otherwise, you may need to remove and replace it.

Kerria japonica   Rosaceae

JAPANESE KERRIA

Thinning out one-third of the oldest stems each year will keep Japanese kerria vigorous and free-blooming. Remove suckers and winter-killed tips as needed.

DESCRIPTION: Japanese kerria is a bushy, deciduous shrub with slender, green branches that hold their color throughout the year. The golden yellow, five-petaled flowers open in mid- to late-spring, giving the plant the appearance of a giant mutant marigold. The cultivar 'Pleniflora' has double flowers. Height to about 6 feet (1.8 m). Japanese kerria grows best in deep, moist, humus-rich soil and partial shade. Zones 4–8.

WHEN TO PRUNE: In late spring or early summer after flowering.

HOW TO PRUNE: Thin by cutting one-third of the oldest stems to ground level. Rejuvenate an overgrown plant by cutting the entire shrub to the ground.

SPECIAL TIPS: Japanese kerria blooms most vigorously when actively growing. Annual thinning will promote strong flowering shoots.

Leucothoe fontanesiana   Ericaceae

DROOPING LEUCOTHOE

Drooping leucothoe has long, graceful, arching stems. Prune each year to remove any winter damage; thin out some of the oldest stems after flowering.

DESCRIPTION: Drooping leucothoe is evergreen with arching branches and dark green leaves that tend to bronze in winter. Its white flowers appear in drooping clusters in midspring. Height to 6 feet (1.8 m). Like rhododendrons, azaleas, and other relatives, leucothoe prefers moist, acid soil and partial shade. Zones 4–9.

WHEN TO PRUNE: In late spring or early summer after flowering.

HOW TO PRUNE: Cut one-third of the oldest or winter-damaged stems to ground level each year.

Ligustrum spp.   Oleaceae

PRIVETS

Privets can tolerate heavy pruning, making them popular for use as screens and hedges. Trim in winter or after flowering for shape; reclaim overgrown plants with drastic pruning.

DESCRIPTION: Privets are upright, deciduous or evergreen shrubs with white flowers in spring, followed by black berries in fall. Privets require full sun and well-drained soil.

  L. amurense (amur privet): Deciduous; height to 15 feet (4.5 m). Zones 4–7.

  L. japonicum (Japanese privet): Evergreen; height 8–12 feet (2.4–3.6 m). Has glossy foliage and pyramidal clusters of white flowers. Zones 7–9.

  L. obtusifolium (border privet): Deciduous; height 10–12 feet (3–3.6 m). Zones 4–7.

WHEN TO PRUNE: If you enjoy the flowers, wait to prune until after flowering; otherwise, prune during the dormant season. Prune hedges as needed throughout the growing season.

HOW TO PRUNE: Trim freestanding shrubs and informal hedges as needed for shape. Thin out crowded stems by cutting a few to the ground or back to another branch. Shear formal hedges as needed. To rejuvenate an overgrown privet, cut it back hard—to a few inches above the ground or to a taller framework of stems—and let it regrow.

SPECIAL TIPS: Privets tolerate heavy pruning. They are widely used for hedges and are sometimes trimmed for fast-growing outdoor topiary projects.

Mahonia spp.   Berberidaceae

MAHONIAS

Annual pruning will encourage mahonias to grow vigorous young stems, producing a full, bushy look. If plants get spindly looking, cut all the stems to the ground to promote new growth.

DESCRIPTION: Mahonias are evergreen, suckering shrubs with compound, holly-like foliage. They grow best in well-drained soil and tolerate some shade. Yellow flowers and waxy, gray-blue fruits provide seasonal interest.

  M. aquifolium (Oregon grape): Has upright stems; height 3–6 feet (90–180 cm). The foliage may bronze in a severe winter. Zones 6–8.

  M. bealei (leather-leaved mahonia): May grow to 12 feet (3.6 m), although usually 4–6 feet (1.2–1.8 m). The flowers appear in late winter and are popular with honeybees that emerge in early spring. The fruits are large and rather grape-like in appearance. In a severe winter, the foliage is likely to display fall color in vibrant reds, oranges, and yellows. Zones 6–8.

WHEN TO PRUNE: In spring after flowering.

HOW TO PRUNE: Cut one-third of the oldest stems to ground level to promote the production of new stems. Rejuvenate an overgrown plant by cutting the entire shrub to the ground.

SPECIAL TIPS: Mahonias get leggy and scraggly if not pruned for vigorous growth.

Myrica pensylvanica   Myricaceae

BAYBERRY

Bayberries usually look great without regular pruning. Trim shoots back lightly if you want to control the shape; you may also choose to remove suckers that come out too far.

DESCRIPTION: Bayberry is a deciduous or semi-evergreen shrub with shiny, fragrant leaves and clusters of white, waxy fruit. It can grow to 9 feet (2.7 m) tall. Native to the seasides of the northeastern coast of North America, it tolerates salt spray and poor soil admirably. Bayberry grows best in full sun to partial shade. Zones 2–7.

WHEN TO PRUNE: Anytime.

HOW TO PRUNE: Bayberries are trouble-free shrubs that seldom need any pruning. If desired, trim lightly with heading cuts to encourage compact growth. Rejuvenate an overgrown plant by pruning heavily during the dormant season.

SPECIAL TIPS: Some bayberry plants are males; some are females. Only females bear fruit, but you need both male and female plants to get pollination and fruit. Unfortunately, nurseries rarely sell separate male and female plants. If you really want to be sure, buy plants in fall, and get at least one with fruit and one without.

Nandina domestica   Berberidaceae

HEAVENLY BAMBOO

Pruning out one-third of the oldest stems each year will keep heavenly bamboo bushy and beautiful. Prune in late winter or early spring or in midwinter to use the trimmings indoors.

DESCRIPTION: Heavenly bamboo is not a true bamboo; it is a graceful, evergreen shrub with compound leaves that turn red to purplish bronze in fall. White flowers in midsummer are followed by persistent clusters of red fruit in the fall. It can grow to 10 feet (3 m), but most gardeners keep it shorter—around 4–6 feet (1.2–1.8 m)—with pruning. The cultivar 'Harbour Dwarf' is often used as a groundcover, as it usually only grows 18–24 inches (45–60 cm) high. Heavenly bamboo thrives in both full sun and dense shade; provide deep, moist, well-drained soil. Zones 6–10.

WHEN TO PRUNE: In late winter or early spring before growth begins.

HOW TO PRUNE: Cut one-third of the oldest canes to the ground annually.

SPECIAL TIPS: Some gardeners wait until December to prune and work the trimmings into creative holiday decorations.

| *Philadelphus coronarius* | Saxifragaceae | *Photinia serrulata* | Rosaceae |

SWEET MOCK ORANGE

CHINESE PHOTINIA

To keep sweet mock orange attractive and blooming well, prune one-third of the oldest stems to the ground each year. Reclaim overgrown plants by cutting them to the ground.

Chinese photinia is an adaptable large shrub or small tree with reddish young leaves that age to dark green. A light summer trimming can keep Chinese photinia in bounds.

DESCRIPTION: Sweet mock orange is an upright, arching, rounded shrub that can grow to 12 feet (3.6 m) tall. It is primarily grown for the fragrant white flowers it produces in late spring. The stem bark peels to reveal orange inner bark. The dark green leaves show no fall color. Plants adapt to full sun or partial shade with well-drained but evenly moist soil. Zones 4–9.

WHEN TO PRUNE: Soon after flowering. Don't wait until fall or early spring; you'll cut off the flower buds and lose a whole season of bloom.

HOW TO PRUNE: Cut one-third of the oldest stems to the ground annually. To rejuvenate an overgrown mock orange, cut the entire shrub to the ground.

DESCRIPTION: Chinese photinia is an evergreen shrub that bears showy clusters of white flowers in spring, followed by bright red fruits in fall. The normally green leaves may turn bright red or bronze in fall. Chinese photinia has a rounded habit and can grow to 30 feet (9 m) tall. Provide full sun and well-drained soil. Zones 7–10.

WHEN TO PRUNE: In summer.

HOW TO PRUNE: Trim lightly to encourage compact growth. To rejuvenate an overgrown plant, cut the entire shrub to the ground.

SPECIAL TIPS: Photinia is prone to fire blight, a bacterial disease that causes shoot tips to turn black. Prune off affected stems with at least 6 inches (15 cm) of healthy wood. Dip or wipe shears with isopropyl alcohol between cuts to sanitize them. Destroy the prunings.

Pieris spp.   Ericaceae

PIERIS

Pieris have a naturally dense branching structure that needs little pruning to look attractive. Simply remove dead wood or poorly placed branches after flowering.

DESCRIPTION: These evergreens need partial shade and moist, well-drained, humus-rich soil.
P. *floribunda* (mountain pieris or fetterbush): Has a rounded, spreading habit; height to 6 feet (1.8 m). Upright clusters of creamy white flowers appear in spring. Zones 5–7.
P. *japonica* (Japanese pieris): Height to 10 feet (3 m) under favorable conditions. Creamy white flower clusters cascade from branch tips in spring. Zones 6–7.

WHEN TO PRUNE: In late spring after flowering.

HOW TO PRUNE: Needs little, if any, pruning. Remove spent flower clusters to promote future flower production. Remove dead wood or errant branches at the ground or at the union with another stem.

Pinus mugo   Pinaceae

SWISS MOUNTAIN PINE

Swiss mountain pine can vary widely in height and spread. Pinching or cutting off half of each new shoot will promote lower growth and a bushier habit.

DESCRIPTION: Swiss mountain pine, also commonly known as mugo pine, is a shrub or small tree. The species can grow 15–20 feet (4.5–6 m) tall; the lower, rounded, shrubby cultivars are more popular for landscaping. Swiss mountain pine adapts to many soil types; it grows best in a site with full sun and good drainage. Zones 3–7.

WHEN TO PRUNE: At the "candle" stage, when the new growth on the shoot tips is just beginning to expand.

HOW TO PRUNE: Remove—by pinching or with hand pruners—one-half of the length of each new candle. This promotes fullness by encouraging new shoots to form along the branches and by reducing the total length of the new growth.

SPECIAL TIPS: Cultivars can vary widely in mature size. Pruning as described above will help to keep larger-growing types more compact. See the Pines entry on page 77 for details on pruning tree-type pines.

CHERRY-LAUREL

Cherry-laurel has a wide-spreading habit and glossy evergreen leaves. After flowering, prune one-third of the oldest stems to the ground each year.

DESCRIPTION: Cherry-laurel is neither a true cherry nor a true laurel. This evergreen bears shiny, leathery leaves on arching stems 12–15 feet (3.6–4.5 m) tall. White flowers bloom in the leaf axils in early spring to midspring, followed by black fruits. Unlike most of its relatives in the rose family, cherry-laurel performs best in some shade. It likes steady soil moisture but can't tolerate soggy, poorly drained sites. Zones 6–8.

WHEN TO PRUNE: In late spring after flowering.

HOW TO PRUNE: Cut one-third of the oldest stems to the ground annually.

SPECIAL TIPS: In the South, cherry-laurel is a popular choice for hedges and screens. Trim as needed for shape in spring or summer. Use hand pruners, not hedge shears, when trimming formal hedges to avoid cutting into the leaves.

SCARLET FIRETHORN

As its name suggests, scarlet firethorn is well armed with wicked thorns. Wear heavy gloves as you prune out suckers, watersprouts, and tangled growth after flowering.

DESCRIPTION: Scarlet firethorn is a thorny deciduous shrub with an irregular growth habit. It can grow up to 15 feet (4.5 m) tall. Clusters of small white flowers bloom in spring, followed in fall by orange-red berries that look like rose hips. A popular subject for espalier, firethorn can make a dramatic splash against a wall or trellis. It needs full sun and well-drained soil to perform best. Zones 6–8.

WHEN TO PRUNE: In late spring or early summer after flowering.

HOW TO PRUNE: Wear heavy gloves and long sleeves to protect your hands and arms from the vicious thorns! Thin out crowded and awkward-looking branches to keep the plant's shape. Also remove suckers and watersprouts. Trim firethorn hedges as needed through the growing season.

Rhododendron spp.   Ericaceae

RHODODENDRONS

Most rhododendrons and azaleas need only minimal pruning. Trim evergreen azaleas after flowering to control the size; on others, remove dead wood and trim awkwardly placed branches.

DESCRIPTION: The genus *Rhododendron* includes both rhododendrons and azaleas. Rhododendrons tend to be evergreen, while azaleas are usually deciduous, but there is some overlap. Bloom times vary widely, depending on the species and cultivar. Some, like Korean rhododendron (*R. mucronulatum*) start blooming in late winter; plum-leaved azalea (*R. prunifolium*) blooms as late as August. Most of the hybrids that you'll find at your local garden center will bloom in midspring to early sumer. Rhododendrons and azaleas prefer partial shade, well-drained, humus-rich soil with steady moisture, and a site out of the wind.

WHEN TO PRUNE: In spring or summer after flowering, giving plenty of time for the formation of next year's flower buds.

HOW TO PRUNE: Most rhododendrons and azaleas need little pruning. Remove dead wood and trim awkwardly placed branches back to another stem or to the ground. Head back the shoots of spindly rhododendrons by trimming to just above a lower rosette of leaves on the same stem.

SPECIAL TIPS: For a good show of flowers the following year, remove spent blooms on evergreen rhododendrons before they go to seed. You'll find that the flower clusters break off nicely when you bend them between your thumb and forefinger.

Rhus spp.   Anacardiaceae

SUMACS

To keep older sumacs under control, cut a few of the oldest stems to the ground. Also pull or mow off suckers if they pop up where they're not wanted.

DESCRIPTION: Sumacs are deciduous, upright shrubs or small trees popular for their attractive leaves and outstanding fall color. They tend to sucker and form large colonies if left unmanaged; regular pruning will control their spread. Sumacs adapt well to different soil types, as long as there is good drainage; they can take full sun or partial shade.

R. aromatica (fragrant sumac): Irregular, mounded shrub; height 2–6 feet (60–180 cm). Yellow spring flowers give way to fuzzy red fruits by fall. Fragrant, three-part leaves turn to brilliant reds and oranges in fall. 'Gro-Low' grows no taller than 2 feet (60 cm). Zones 3–9.

R. typhina (staghorn sumac): Shrub or small tree with a loose, open branching habit; height 15–25 feet (4.5–7.5 m). Compound leaves turn red and orange in the fall. Fuzzy red fruits provide food for the birds. Zones 3–8.

WHEN TO PRUNE: In late winter or early spring before growth begins.

HOW TO PRUNE: Cut the oldest stems to the ground if the plant starts to get out of bounds; otherwise, sumacs need little pruning.

SPECIAL TIPS: If the word "sumac" makes you itch, bear in mind that the notorious poison sumac (*Rhus vernix*) occupies swampy sites and has white berries. The species described here pose none of the hazards of their swampy cousin.

Spiraea spp.   Rosaceae

SPIREAS

Keep spireas vigorous and free-blooming by cutting one-third of the oldest stems to the ground each year. Reclaim overgrown plants by pruning all stems to just above the ground.

DESCRIPTION: Spireas are deciduous shrubs with white or pink flowers in mid- to late spring. They look great in flower borders, shrub borders, and informal hedges. Spireas require full sun and good drainage.

    S. x *bumalda* (Bumald spirea): Has a low, mounded, twiggy form; height to 2 feet (60 cm). Small white to deep pink flowers bloom in flat clusters. Zones 4–8.

    S. prunifolia (bridalwreath spirea): Has an upright, mounded form; height to 10 feet (3 m). Double white flowers bloom along the length of each branch. Zones 5–8.

    S. x *vanhouttei* (Vanhoutte spirea): Has an arching form with some bareness at the base; height 6–8 feet (2.4–3.2 m). White flowers bloom in flat clusters along the branches; the foliage is blue-green. Zones 3–8.

WHEN TO PRUNE: Prune Bumald spirea during the dormant season; prune all others after flowering.

HOW TO PRUNE: Cut one-third of the oldest stems to the ground each year. If plants are overgrown and need drastic renewal, prune all the stems to a few inches above the ground.

Syringa spp.   Oleaceae

LILACS

Lilacs tend to get scrawny and may flower less without regular pruning. Encourage strong growth by pruning out a few of the oldest stems after flowering each year.

DESCRIPTION: Lilacs are deciduous shrubs or small trees beloved for their fragrant spring flowers. Grow them individually as specimen plants or plant several together as an informal hedge. Lilacs perform best in full sun and well-drained soil.

    S. laciniata (cut-leaved lilac): Has a rounded, arching form; height about 6 feet (1.8 m). Deeply lobed leaves give the plant a fine texture. Fragrant lavender flowers bloom in loose clusters along the branches. Zones 5–8.

    S. meyeri (Meyer lilac): Broad shrub; height to 8 feet (2.4 m). Lightly fragrant, violet-purple flowers cover the plant in spring. Zones 4–8.

    S. vulgaris (common lilac): Upright, vase-shaped form; height to 20 feet (6 m). The purplish or white fragrant flowers bloom in clusters on stem tips. Zones 3–7.

WHEN TO PRUNE: In late spring after flowering.

HOW TO PRUNE: To encourage profuse flowering, remove spent blooms. To keep a lilac growing and blooming vigorously, remove a few of the oldest stems just above ground level each year. Cultivars are sometimes grafted onto privet or common lilac, so consider removing suckers as they appear; otherwise, you may end up with a privet or common lilac and not the cultivar you originally selected.

| *Taxus* spp. | Taxaceae | *Thuja occidentalis* | Cupressaceae |

YEWS

AMERICAN ARBORVITAE

Yews respond well to shearing in spring to midsummer, so they're popular for formal hedges. Plants can be equally attractive if you let them grow into their natural forms.

American arborvitae cultivars vary widely in size and shape. Choose the right one for your needs and give the plants plenty of room and they'll rarely need pruning.

DESCRIPTION: Yews are needle-leaved evergreens. Some species can reach tree size, but yews are most commonly grown as shrubs. They require steady soil moisture, perfect drainage, and full sun to partial shade.

T. baccata (English yew): Has deep green foliage and a graceful demeanor. Tree forms may grow to 50 feet (15 m); most commonly grown cultivars are shrubs that grow 4–6 feet (1.2–1.8 m) tall. 'Repandens' is a low, spreading shrub; height to about 3 feet (90 cm). Zones 6–7.

T. cuspidata (Japanese yew): Shrub or tree; height 4–40 feet (1.2–12 m). The cultivar 'Capitata' is a popular pyramidal form. Zones 4–7.

T. x *media* (Anglojapanese yew): Includes cultivars in numerous shapes and sizes; height 2–20 feet (60 cm–6 m). Zones 5–7.

WHEN TO PRUNE: In spring or summer.

HOW TO PRUNE: Many forms have a naturally attractive shape and don't need regular pruning. Simply trim to shape by removing errant branches at the ground or where they join another branch. Shear formal hedges as needed throughout the growing season; stop by midsummer to give new growth time to harden off before cold weather. Reclaim overgrown or badly pruned plants by cutting the stems back to a framework of branches about 1–2 feet (30–60 cm) above the ground.

DESCRIPTION: Arborvitaes are scaly-leaved evergreen shrubs or trees with rather vertical, fan-like foliage that's aromatic when crushed. Shrubby cultivars such as 'Globe' or 'Golden Globe' are round in outline; height to about 4 feet (1.2 m). The species can grow to 60 feet (18 m). Intermediate cultivars are 'Emerald', with a pyramidal form and height to 15 feet (4.5 m), and 'Techny', with an upright oval form and height to 30 feet (9 m). Give both cultivars full sun and soil with steady moisture and good drainage. Zones 3–7.

WHEN TO PRUNE: During the dormant season. Shear hedges as needed through the growing season.

HOW TO PRUNE: Plants seldom need pruning. To retain the natural form of the plant, selectively remove branches as needed. Cut back to another branch or clump of foliage; don't leave stubs. Shear formal hedges lightly; avoid cutting back into the bare wood. Arborvitae tolerates hard pruning only when it's young and growing vigorously; older stems won't resprout.

SPECIAL TIPS: Cultivars vary widely in mature size; read the tags on plants at your local nursery to find the cultivars that will fit in the space you have available. Cultivars such as 'Globe' and 'Emerald' give gardeners the option of growing this appealing evergreen without having to fight with its natural tendency to become large.

Tsuga spp.   Pinaceae   *Viburnum* spp.   Caprifoliaceae

HEMLOCKS   # VIBURNUMS

Hemlocks can tolerate the frequent spring or summer shearing that's needed to shape a formal hedge. For less maintenance, consider a more informal hemlock screen.

DESCRIPTION: Hemlocks are graceful, needle-leaved evergreens with a loosely pyramidal form and a soft texture. The tip often nods away from prevailing winds. Hemlocks prefer cool climates and moist, humus-rich, well-drained soil. They can take full sun in the North but appreciate light shade in warm areas. They are not very tolerant of sites exposed to high winds, salt, or pollution. Unlike other evergreens, hemlocks tolerate heavy pruning; they are attractive in either formal or informal hedges and screens.

T. canadensis (Canada or eastern hemlock): Can grow to a height of 75 feet (22.5 m), although 30 feet (9 m) is more likely in the landscape. Trimming will, of course, keep plants even shorter. Zones 3–8.

T. caroliniana (Carolina hemlock): Has blunter needles and, generally, a deeper green color; height to 75 feet (22.5 m) when untrimmed. Zones 5–7.

WHEN TO PRUNE: In spring or summer.

HOW TO PRUNE: Hemlocks are particularly beautiful in loose, informal screens; these will need little or no trimming. For a more formal hedge, shear as needed through the growing season. Make your last shearing by midsummer, so any new growth can harden off before cold weather arrives.

SPECIAL TIPS: See the Hemlocks entry on page 82 for details on handling tree-form hemlocks.

After your viburnums bloom each year, cut one-third of the oldest stems to the ground. This will encourage more compact growth and good flower and fruit production.

DESCRIPTION: Viburnums are deciduous or evergreen, spring-blooming shrubs or trees. The fruits, which ripen in the fall, are often popular with birds. Fall color is outstanding in some species. Give viburnums full sun to partial shade and evenly moist but well-drained soil.

V. dentatum (arrowwood viburnum): One of the more upright, suckering shrub-type viburnums. White flowers—fragrant in some species—appear in late spring to early summer, followed by fruits that turn blue or black by fall. Zones 4–8.

V. plicatum var. *tomentosum* (doublefile viburnum): Popular deciduous, rounded shrub with a horizontally layered growing habit; height 8–10 feet (2.4–3 m). Flat, 3-inch (7.5 cm) clusters of small white flowers, ringed by larger, sterile blooms, appear in pairs along each branch. In the fall, fruits formed from the fertile flowers turn from red to black, and the foliage turns a dull red. Zones 5–8.

WHEN TO PRUNE: After flowering.

HOW TO PRUNE: Cut one-third of the oldest growth to the ground annually. Remove vertical watersprouts as they appear on doublefile viburnum; they ruin the horizontal grace of this plant.

SPECIAL TIPS: In a severe winter, the stems and leaves of evergreen viburnums may turn brown. Prune damaged shoots by selectively removing stems at the base of the plant.

Weigela florida   Caprifoliaceae

OLD-FASHIONED WEIGELA

The stem tips of old-fashioned weigelas often die back in winter; prune damaged wood out after flowering. Also cut out one-third of the oldest stems each year.

DESCRIPTION: Old-fashioned weigela is a spreading, shrub that grows 6–10 feet (1.8–3 m) tall. It is mainly grown for it bell-shaped, 1^1/$_2$-inch (3.7 cm), rose-colored spring flowers. 'Bristol Snowflake' is a white-flowered cultivar. 'Centennial' and 'Dropmore Pink' are hardy to Zone 3; most cultivars are adapted to Zones 4–8.

WHEN TO PRUNE: After flowering.

HOW TO PRUNE: Dieback may be a problem following a severe winter; prune out this wood first. Each year, thin out the plant by removing about one-third of the oldest stems close to ground level. Head back stray branches to maintain the plant's shape.

Yucca spp.   Agavaceae

YUCCAS

Yuccas form sturdy clumps of stiff, pointed, or spine-tipped leaves. To keep them looking their best, cut spent flower stalks down to the leaves after blooming and remove dead leaves.

DESCRIPTION: Yuccas are evergreen shrubs or groundcovers. They form stout clumps of swordlike leaves; the leaves often have hair-like filaments curling off the margins. The upright flower stalks appear in early summer and can grow to 10 feet (3 m) or more. These stalks bear pendant, creamy white 2-inch (5 cm) flowers that are soon followed by seedpods. Yuccas need full sun and good drainage; they can take heat, high humidity, and drought. Zones 4–9.

WHEN TO PRUNE: After flowering.

HOW TO PRUNE: Cut dead leaves and flower stalks off at the base.

SPECIAL TIPS: Use yuccas with caution, as the stiff leaves can be sharply pointed. They are not a great choice for planting around kids' play areas or along paths where they may attack passersby!

PRUNING TREES

Your trees need all the help and understanding they can get from you to stay healthy. Stresses from soil compaction, root zone disturbance, poor placement, vandalism, and pollution—in every possible combination—challenge trees in most environments where humans have made their mark. Even the most hospitable planting environments are disturbed in some way, altered from a more natural state by our presence and activities. Human activities that interfere with normal tree growth also make the trees more prone to their natural enemies, including a variety of pest and disease problems.

What does this have to do with pruning? A key part of maintaining any tree successfully is understanding how that tree grows, what it needs to grow to its potential, and how it will respond to the pruning you do. Choosing a tree that is adapted to your growing conditions is the first step toward future tree health. Following through with careful site selection, good maintenance, and proper pruning—especially during the first few years—will help the tree withstand many of the stresses it will be exposed to throughout its life.

The few minutes you routinely put into tree care is cheap insurance against future problems. Poorly chosen, abused, or neglected trees may have branches that drop off or may fall over completely, exacting a toll that can include loss of life, personal injury, property damage, great expense, and inconveniences ranging from lawsuits to power failures to impeded travel. Fear of this kind of damage, accompanied by a lack of understanding of how trees grow, has led many people to pruning practices that are self-defeating. Topping, for instance, is a practice that removes most of a tree's crown, perhaps making it look safer to the untrained eye. But topping disfigures and weakens the tree, leaving it ultimately more dangerous—and more costly—than if it had been left to grow naturally.

Leaving a tree completely untouched isn't an option in our communities and neighborhoods. Unless you move into a house with a bare lot, you'll be dealing with trees that were planted by the builder or the previous owner, and these trees may not have been well chosen or well pruned. With some care from you, though, they can grow and develop into strong, beautiful additions to your landscape.

This chapter is your guide to pruning trees with some understanding of how they grow and how they will respond to the cuts you make. The "Guide to Trees," starting on page 62, offers specifics on when and how to prune 43 common shade trees, flowering trees, and evergreens. Besides leaving you with healthy, beautiful landscape plants, this kind of informed, effective pruning offers results that are economical, long-lasting, and ultimately very satisfying.

Pruning isn't just a chore you have to do to keep plants a certain size or shape. Good pruning can also help your plants look their best by accentuating the natural branching habit and exposing beautiful bark.

As you train young trees, you may choose to remove one or two of the lowest branches each year to make it easier to walk or mow around the base.

Tree Pruning Basics

Careful pruning throughout a tree's life will go a long way toward keeping it strong and healthy. Here are some guidelines on when and how to prune.

Pruning at Planting Time

A few careful cuts at planting time will get your young tree off to a good start. Before planting, trim any dead or damaged roots on bare-root stock back to healthy-looking tissue. After planting, any tree will benefit if you prune out:

- Dead, dying, or damaged stems or branches.
- Broken, crossing, or rubbing branches.
- Developing watersprouts and sucker growth.

This is also a good time to look for and start correcting potential structural flaws, such as:

- Two main stems where there is normally just one (remove one).
- More than one branch coming out from a single spot on the trunk (thin them out to leave one).
- Branches that join the trunk at an angle less than 45 degrees (remove any, starting with the narrowest angles first).

You may not be able to do all the pruning your new tree needs at this time. Overall, you don't want to remove more than one-third of the top growth at planting time. If you have removed this much growth and the tree still needs work, save the rest for the next pruning season.

Training a Young Deciduous Tree

The first several years of a tree's life are critical "make or break" years for its future structural stability. During these early years, just a few minutes of pruning each year (easy pruning—the kind you do with hand pruners and loppers while standing on the ground!) can save hours of expensive aerial work done later by a contractor. This early training is also the best prevention there is against future hazards, like weak, dropping branches.

On most deciduous trees, late winter is perfect for this kind of pruning. You'll be able to see the tree's structure more readily and work more quickly with the leaves off of the tree. The tree is also getting ready to start active growth, a time when it can most quickly recover from pruning wounds. For trees that are likely to bleed sap when pruned in late winter or early spring (see "Bleeding Trees" on page 57 for a list), choose summer or fall instead for annual pruning.

When you are ready to start pruning, follow these simple steps:

1. Remove dead or dying wood, as well as suckers and watersprouts.

2. Prune out any poorly placed stems that are crossing, rubbing against each other, or pointing in toward the center of the plant.

3. If the tree has two main leaders instead of just one, use a thinning cut to remove one.

4. Walk around the tree and look at the arrangement

Neglected young trees can develop serious flaws as they mature.

Pruning a young tree carefully will give you a safe, handsome mature tree.

If you have the room, you may decide to allow the lower branches to sweep the ground for a graceful look.

of the main branches from all sides. They should be spaced evenly around and up the trunk. If two or more branches originate close to each other on the trunk, keep the best-placed one and prune out the others.

5. Check for narrow branch crotches, especially on trees like 'Bradford' callery pear (*Pyrus calleryana* 'Bradford'), American yellowwood (*Cladrastis lutea*), and Japanese zelkova (*Zelkova serrata*). Narrow branch angles (less than 45 degrees) are inherently weaker than wider angles, and they tend to split under the pressure of heavy wind, rain, or snow. On young trees, selectively remove branches with narrow crotches in favor of those with wider angles.

6. Finally, consider a little thinning to open the tree's crown to sun and air. This reduces wind drag on the branches, reduces surface area for the accumulation of rain and snow, helps to discourage fungal diseases, and improves flowering.

Pruning the "Weed" Trees

Fast-growing trees like poplars and silver maples may be good for quick shade or screening, but they can become a menace as they mature. The following trees tend to have soft, weak wood, making them prone to drop limbs broken by strong winds, rain, or snow:

Acer negundo (box elder)
Acer saccharinum (silver maple)
Ailanthus altissima (tree-of-heaven)
Albizia julibrissin (mimosa)
Morus spp. (mulberries)
Populus spp. (poplars)
Ulmus pumila (Siberian elm)

With careful pruning during their formative stages (as explained in "Training a Young Deciduous Tree" on page 56), weak-wooded trees may develop into respectable landscape specimens that grace your landscape for years to come. If your property has a larger, unpruned tree of the kinds listed above, it's worth having an arborist come to evaluate the tree's health. The tree may be fine or just need a little pruning to reduce the hazard of dropping branches. If the tree is really in poor shape, the arborist may advise that you have the tree removed for the safety of your home and family.

Bleeding Trees

There are a few trees that tend to "bleed" sap if pruned in late winter or early spring. While this oozing sap doesn't pose any danger to the tree, some people find it to be undesirable, especially where cars are parked. To avoid this, prune the following trees in summer or fall:

Acer spp. (maples)
Betula spp. (birches)
Cladrastis lutea (American yellowwood)
Cornus spp. (dogwoods)
Juglans spp. (walnuts)
Ulmus spp. (elms)

Limbs that cross and rub can cause wounds, which are prime targets for pests and diseases. Remove one of the limbs.

If your tree is large enough that you'd need a ladder to prune it, it's time to call a professional arborist.

Trimming Evergreen Trees

Evergreen trees require remarkably little pruning. Use heading cuts to encourage a loose, open evergreen to fill in; use thinning cuts to open one that's too dense. Be careful not to trim the central leader, as losing it means that your evergreen tree will become fat and bushy rather than upright. If the leader does get damaged by pests, pruning, or storms, see the Firs entry on page 62 to learn about a technique that restores central leaders to evergreens that have lost them.

Pruning Palms

Prune palms when dropping fronds, fruit, or leaf stalks (petioles) may be dangerous to people or property below. Remove only those fronds with petioles that join the top of the crown at an angle greater than 45 degrees. Take out no more than 20 percent of the live fronds in any one growing season. Cut close to the base of the leaf stalk, but be careful not to damage the trunk. To remove dead fronds, try peeling them from the trunk. If a leaf doesn't peel away easily, cut it off instead; otherwise, you may damage the trunk.

Maintaining Mature Trees

Pruning large trees is a heavy-duty job that needs the expertise and equipment of a professional arborist. "Picking a Professional Arborist" on page 60 offers guidelines on choosing a good tree service. But even though you can't do the pruning yourself, you can help to keep your trees sound and healthy by inspecting them regularly and getting small problems corrected early.

All you need is the pruning eye that you developed while learning to train young trees (see "Training a Young Deciduous Tree" on page 56) and a few minutes per plant. You can inspect mature trees any time of

---

Removing Larger Limbs

As your trees mature, pruners and loppers may not be strong enough to do the work you need. When you begin to deal with branches larger than 1½ inches (3.7 cm) in diameter, it's time to start using a pruning saw. With a good saw and a proper three-point cut, you'll be able to remove the limbs you need to with minimal danger to the tree. Follow these steps:

Make the first cut with a handsaw or chainsaw on the underside of the limb, 1 to 2 feet (30 to 60 cm) out from the trunk. Saw halfway through the limb.

Make the second cut on the top of the limb, about 1 inch (2.5 cm) farther out toward the branch tip. The limb will break between the two cuts.

Finish by making a clean straight cut with the saw just outside the branch collar. You may want to support the stub with your free hand as you cut.

On evergreen trees, you can prune out dead, damaged, or dying branches anytime during the year.

Large trees are an asset in any landscape, but they can turn into a liability if not properly maintained.

the year, but the dormant season is the easiest time to spot structural problems (usually the biggest concern). Look for signs of any of the following problems:
• Narrow crotches supporting heavy branches.
• Two main leaders where there should only be one.
• Large crossing or rubbing branches.
• Dense growth that can catch wind, rain, or snow.
If you spot any of these features, it's time to call in a professional tree service. They may suggest one or more of the following types of pruning to make trees safer and easier to live with.

Crown Lifting Also commonly known as limbing up, crown lifting removes tree limbs on the lower part of the trunk. This makes it easier and safer for you to walk, play, and mow around the tree.

Crown Thinning Selectively removing side branches in the crown of the tree reduces weight on the limbs and allows air to move through more easily. Thinning also reduces weight loads from rain and snow and discourages fungal diseases by improving air circulation through the crown.

Crown Reduction A combination of techniques—including selective thinning and drop-crotch cuts—can safely and effectively reduce a tree's crown by up to one-third. Careful crown reduction retains the natural character of the tree, unlike topping, which destroys it.

Storm Proofing This method uses a variety of techniques to reduce a tree's wind resistance. It also involves balancing the weight of the crown in such a way that if the tree does fall, it should fall away from where it would do the most damage.

Limbing Up

As you prune your young tree, think about the activities that are likely to go on around and beneath the tree, then decide if you wish to keep or remove lower limbs. Mowing, recreation, traffic, and pedestrian use all indicate that some limbing up might be in order. Do this gradually. Experience has shown that those lower limbs are important to the developing girth of the trunk, so removing them too soon means a skinny, weak trunk.

A good rule of thumb is to remove one or two of the lower limbs annually, starting with the lowest. As you remove these limbs, be sure to leave the branch collar; do not cut the limbs off flush with the trunk. As your young tree begins to mature, those last lower limbs may be large and heavy enough that you will need to use a three-point cut; see "Removing Larger Limbs" for complete details.

If your tree needs pruning that you can't do from the ground with pole pruners, it's best to hire a professional.

Picking a Professional Arborist

When finances are tight, it can be tempting to put off calling in a professional arborist. But for best results, you should consider large trees to be like any other major component of your home; they need to be inspected and maintained regularly to prevent expensive problems and hazards from popping up. Over time, regular professional maintenance will keep your trees growing safely and healthy, at a minimum cost to you. Fortunately, the job of choosing an arborist has been made considerably easier in recent years with the adoption of national certification and standards for arborists and their work.

What Can an Arborist Do for You?

One thing is certain: Pruning a large tree is a job for a professional who has the equipment and experience to do the job safely and effectively. Professional arborists are well equipped to handle crown reduction, crown lifting, and other tasks described in "Maintaining Mature Trees" on page 58.

In addition to pruning, arborists usually offer a wide variety of services related to the health care of trees. These services may include soil aeration, tree moving, "surgery" such as cabling and bracing, and lightning protection. Professionals may also offer fertilization and pest control services, but they generally use synthetic fertilizers and pesticides. Look for a company that is willing to use organic materials if you plan to use these services.

When to Call a Pro

Use this checklist to help you decide if you need to call in an arborist. Professionals should handle:

- Any cut that you can't make from the ground with pole pruners.
- Any cut that you can't comfortably or confidently make with pole pruners, even though you can reach it.
- Any chain saw cut that requires you to reach above shoulder level.
- Any work—whether you can reach it or not—in a tree near power lines.
- Crown work on large trees, including thinning, raising, reducing, and storm proofing.
- Storm damage repair where heavy limbs are still attached or hung up in the crown or crotches of a tree.
- Cabling, bracing, or any other "surgery."

How to Find a Qualified Arborist

The International Society of Arboriculture (ISA) now has a certification program for arborists in the United States and Canada. Certified arborists have passed tests that demonstrate their knowledge of tree botany, diagnosis, maintenance practices, safety, and other

Removing large dead or dying trees is definitely not a job for an amateur. A pro will do the job safely and cleanly.

Don't wait until your tree is in trouble to call an arborist; have young trees trained right from the start.

related disciplines. While certification holds no guarantees, it represents a significant improvement in a trade where it was once difficult to determine a contractor's proficiency. You can find an ISA-certified arborist near you by calling the ISA at (217) 355-9411. Other ways to judge the qualifications of an arborist or tree service are discussed below.

Telephone Listings Although anyone can advertise in the yellow pages, a listing in a phone book indicates some degree of permanence.

Insurance Carrying liability insurance for personal and property damage, as well as workmen's compensation, is standard practice for conscientious tree services. Professionals will quickly and willingly produce proof of their coverage. Bear in mind that an uninsured tree service working on your property is a liability to you.

Local References Competent professionals are always happy to let you see their work and to put you in touch with other customers who can provide a reference.

Estimates In some areas, you may need to pay for an estimate, but get one—or two—in writing. If you define the work using standard terminology (discussed below), you can compare "apples to apples" on competing estimates.

Standards to Help You Communicate

In recent years, the National Arborist Association (NAA) and the American National Standards Institute (ANSI) have worked together to produce *Standard Practices for Trees, Shrubs, and Other Woody Plant Maintenance*, ANSI A300. Expected to be fully adopted in the mid-1990s, the standards will prove to be a boon to both arborists and their customers. This document sets out rationale and methods for pruning, defines pruning cuts, and specifically describes types of pruning for large trees. These standard terms will be useful to you when talking to an arborist and contracting for the work that needs to be done. You'll understand what kind of work you're paying for and what kind of results you can expect. For more information on the NAA standards, contact the National Arborist Association, Inc., P.O. Box 1094, Amherst, NH 03031, or call (603) 673-3311.

Losing a large tree can be heartbreaking. Reduce the risk of damage with careful plant selection and proper pruning.

Abies spp.   Pinaceae

FIRS

Firs have a naturally pyramidal habit that seldom needs pruning. Trim only to correct structural problems, like multiple or lost leaders (tip shoots).

DESCRIPTION: Firs are large, pyramidal trees bearing fragrant, evergreen needles. They grow best in full sun and moist, well-drained, acid soil.

A. *balsamea* (balsam fir): Prefers cool climates; height to 75 feet (22.5 m). Zones 2–5.

A. *concolor* (white fir): Slightly more heat-tolerant than balsam fir; height to about 50 feet (15 m) in the landscape. Zones 4–7.

A. *fraseri* (Fraser fir): Grown widely as Christmas trees; height to 40 feet (12 m). Zones 5–6.

WHEN TO PRUNE: Anytime.

HOW TO PRUNE: Firs require little pruning, so less is best unless you have a problem to correct. For instance, it's important to keep one main leader (tip shoot); otherwise, your tree will become more like a large bush. If you lose the leader—storms, insects, and birds are the most common culprits— you can train a new one for the job. Select a branch tip closest to the top of the tree and—if it isn't already vertical—"splint" it to the main trunk to make it vertical. To splint a branch, use typical staking supplies such as a garden stake and some twist-ties or cloth strips. Lightly trim the nearby branches to the typical pyramidal shape of the tree, making sure not to prune the tip being splinted. Check the splint every few weeks to make sure the ties don't strangle or rub the new shoot. You should be able to remove the splint in about a year.

| Acer spp. | Aceraceae | Aesculus spp. | Hippocastanaceae |

MAPLES

HORSE CHESTNUTS

Avoid trimming maples in late winter to spring, when pruning cuts will "bleed" sap; this isn't harmful to the tree, but most gardeners find it undesirable.

Good training when plants are young will help horse chestnuts grow up to be strong mature trees. Prune in winter or after flowering to keep a sturdy main trunk.

DESCRIPTION: Maples are popular deciduous shade trees. They prefer full sun to partial shade and—with the exception of red maple—good drainage.

A. palmatum (Japanese maple): Wonderfully sculptural small tree with multiple trunks; height to about 20 feet (6 m). Zones 5–8; may need shelter from wind in cold Zones.

A. platanoides (Norway maple): Single trunk; height to 50 feet (15 m). Its dense shade and shallow roots make it difficult to grow anything beneath this tree; also reseeds prolifically. Zones 4–6.

A. rubrum (red maple): Normally has a single trunk; height to 60 feet (18 m). Seedling trees can vary in height, hardiness, and fall color. Tolerates wet sites. Zones 3–8.

A. saccharinum (silver maple): Height to 70 feet (21 m). This weak-wooded tree quickly turns into a liability as weak crotches split away under the weight of heavy branches. Zones 3–9.

A. saccharum (sugar maple): Single trunk; height to 70 feet (21 m). Its fall color is legendary. Avoid planting in urban conditions where heat and pollution can stress the tree. Zones 3–7.

WHEN TO PRUNE: In fall to midwinter. Avoid in late winter to spring, as cuts will "bleed" as sap flows.

HOW TO PRUNE: Most maples need little or no pruning. Train the larger maples for a strong central leader and well-distributed side branches.

DESCRIPTION: Horse chestnuts are deciduous trees commonly grown for shade and their showy clusters of spring flowers. They prefer full sun and well-drained, moist soil.

A. x carnea (red horse chestnut): Round-headed tree; height to 40 feet (12 m). Bears spikes of red flowers in midspring. Zones 5–7.

A. glabra (Ohio buckeye): Pale yellow flowers in spring; height to about 35 feet (10.5 m). Fall brings yellow or orange leaf color as well as the "buckeyes" (seeds) for which it is known. Zones 4–6.

A. hippocastanum (common horse chestnut): Blotched white flower clusters appear in mid- to late-spring; height to 75 feet (22.5 m). Zones 4–6.

A. octandra (yellow buckeye): Yellow flowers in mid- to late-spring; height 60–70 feet (18–21 m). Zones 5–7.

WHEN TO PRUNE: In the dormant season or summer, after flowering.

HOW TO PRUNE: Train young trees to a strong central leader. Remove branches that join the trunk at a narrow angle, along with crossing or rubbing branches.

Amelanchier spp.   Rosaceae

SERVICEBERRIES

Serviceberries form attractive large shrubs or small trees with little or no pruning. If fire blight causes brown, burnt-looking tips, trim damaged shoots back into healthy wood.

DESCRIPTION: Serviceberries are deciduous large shrubs or small trees. These four-season landscape plants offer white flowers in spring, edible fruits in summer, beautiful color in fall, and attractive bark in winter. Serviceberries grow best in full sun or partial shade, with moist, well-drained soil.

A. arborea (downy serviceberry): Height to about 20 feet (6 m). The leaves open in spring with a silvery sheen after the white, billowy, fragrant flowers. Edible fruits—looking much like blueberries—appear in early summer, maturing from a reddish to a bluish purple color. Fall color can range from orange to red. Zones 3–8.

A. laevis (Allegheny serviceberry): Similar in many ways to the downy serviceberry except that it lacks the downy silver color in its opening foliage; height to 40 feet (12 m). Zones 3–7.

WHEN TO PRUNE: In spring after flowering.

HOW TO PRUNE: Serviceberries generally need little pruning. On tree forms, train to a central leader while the plant is young. Use thinning cuts to remove dead, dying, crossing, or rubbing branches. To rejuvenate overgrown shrub forms, cut all the stems to ground level.

Betula spp.   Betulaceae

BIRCHES

Give birches a clear space to grow straight up and they'll rarely—if ever—need to be trimmed. If you do need to prune, do it in summer to avoid "bleeding" sap.

DESCRIPTION: Birches are single- or multiple-trunked deciduous trees that are often grown for their attractive bark. They prefer light shade and evenly moist soil. A "cool root run"—shaded roots, humus-rich soil, and generous mulch—is important, especially for the canoe birch.

B. papyrifera (canoe birch): Height to 70 feet (21 m). Known for its white bark with strong black markings. Yellow fall color. Not for hot climates, where insect pests are always a problem; this birch grows best in Zones 2–6.

B. nigra (river birch): Can grow to 40 feet (12 m) in the landscape. Shredding, salmon pink bark; clear yellow fall color. Often planted in groups for great landscape effect. Native to rich bottomlands that flood frequently; a natural for soggy soil, but does not demand it. Zones 4–8.

WHEN TO PRUNE: In summer to avoid "bleeding" sap.

HOW TO PRUNE: Train to a central leader. Needs little else except for the occasional removal of a crossing, rubbing, or otherwise misplaced branch.

Carpinus spp.   Betulaceae

HORNBEAMS

Hornbeams are slow-growing with a naturally graceful form that doesn't need much pruning. Simply remove dead, damaged, or poorly placed branches in late winter or early spring.

DESCRIPTION: Hornbeams are small- to medium-sized deciduous trees grown for their often rippled gray bark and easy-care nature. They prefer moist, well-drained, humus-rich soil.

C. betulus (European hornbeam): Has a dense, upright oval form; height to 50 feet (15 m). Prefers full sun. Zones 5–7.

C. caroliniana (American hornbeam): Has an open, upright form; height to 30 feet (9 m) in the landscape. This native grows best in partial shade. Zones 5–8.

WHEN TO PRUNE: In late winter or early spring before new growth begins.

HOW TO PRUNE: Hornbeams rarely need pruning because of their regular form. Remove only dead, dying, crossing, rubbing, or other errant branches. Use thinning cuts, leaving no stubs. See the European hornbeam entry on page 35 for tips on how to use it as a hedge.

SPECIAL TIPS: This genus is known for its unusually hard wood and tight grain. Be sure your tools are sharp!

Catalpa spp.   Bignoniaceae

CATALPAS

Catalpas are fast-growing, so it's important to train young trees well. In late winter or early spring or after flowering, prune to develop a strong trunk and sturdy branch structure.

DESCRIPTION: Catalpas are single-trunked deciduous trees with large, elephant-ear leaves, white spikes of spotted flowers in spring, and long, slender, pendant seedpods in fall. Catalpas have an open, irregular form that makes them picturesque additions to a large landscape. Plant in full sun with well-drained soil.

C. bignonioides (southern catalpa): Height 30–40 feet (9–12 m). Zones 5–8.

C. speciosa (northern catalpa): Height 40–60 feet (12–18 m). Zones 4–8.

WHEN TO PRUNE: In late winter or early spring before growth begins or in summer after flowering.

HOW TO PRUNE: Catalpas require little pruning. Train young catalpas to a central leader; cut out crossing or rubbing branches and those that join the trunk at a narrow angle. Prune older trees only to eliminate an errant branch or structural defect.

Cedrus spp.   Pinaceae   *Cercis* spp.   Leguminosae

CEDARS   # REDBUDS

Cedars have a beautiful growth habit that doesn't demand lots of pruning. Give these plants plenty of room to develop to their potential and you'll have little work to do!

Redbuds will produce masses of colorful spring flowers without much pruning. Once they are done blooming for the season, prune to remove dead stems and to keep the tree open to sunlight.

DESCRIPTION: Cedars are evergreen trees that tend to be pyramidal in youth and flat-topped, picturesque, and horizontally layered with age. The needles on these evergreens grow from short, compact growths (called spurs) along the branches. Upright waxy cones sit on the branches like candles. Grow cedars in sunny, well-drained conditions.

C. atlantica (Atlas cedar): Height to 60 feet (18 m). 'Glauca' is a cultivar known for its stunning blue needles. Zones 6–9.

C. deodara (deodar cedar): Has soft needles and a weeping habit. The tip of the tree tends to nod to one side. Height to 70 feet (21 m). Zones 7–9. The cultivar 'Kasmir' is known for its cold-hardiness into Zone 6.

C. libani (cedar-of-Lebanon): Bears deep green needles; height to 60 feet (18 m). Zones 5–7.

WHEN TO PRUNE: Anytime.

HOW TO PRUNE: Cedars naturally develop a beautiful form, so they rarely need pruning. Be sure to maintain a single central leader so the tree will keep growing upright. If the central leader gets broken or damaged, see the Firs entry on page 62 in this chapter for tips on creating a new one.

DESCRIPTION: Redbuds are small deciduous trees that bloom in early spring, before their leaves open. Magenta flowers appear on the branches as well as on the trunk. The flowers are followed by papery pods in fall. Plant in full sun or light shade on a site with well-drained soil.

C. canadensis (Eastern redbud): Height 20–30 feet (6–9 m). Its lowest branches are often close to the ground. Zones 4–8.

C. chinensis (Chinese redbud): Smaller than Eastern redbud, it has a height to about 10 feet (3 m). It blooms with or slightly ahead of Eastern redbud. 'Alba' bears white flowers. Zones 6–9.

WHEN TO PRUNE: In spring after flowering.

HOW TO PRUNE: Redbuds need little pruning. Use thinning cuts to remove dead, dying, crossing, or rubbing branches.

Chamaecyparis spp.　　　　　　Cupressaceae

FALSE CYPRESS

Like most evergreen trees, false cypresses don't need much pruning to look great. Just trim in spring to remove awkward branches or to correct a damaged leader (tip shoot).

DESCRIPTION: These evergreens bear tufted, often fan-like foliage. They prefer moist soil, full sun or partial shade, and a site out of the direct wind.
　　C. lawsoniana (Lawson false cypress, Port Orford cedar): Has a pyramidal form; height to 60 feet (18 m) or more. Ascending branches bearing pendant branchlets give this tree a distinctive character. Performs best in moist climates; Zones 5–7.
　　C. nootkatensis (nootka false cypress, Alaska cedar): Conical form with drooping branches. Height may exceed 100 feet (30 m) in its native, cool, moist, coastal climates; reaches only about 15 feet (4.5 m) in warmer climates. Zones 5–7.
　　C. obtusa (Hinoki false cypress): May grow to 50 feet (15 m). Typically, the leaves are formed in closely pressed fans of deep green. Various cultivars within the species offer countless variations of color, shape, and size. Zones 4–8.
　　C. pisifera (Sawara false cypress): Has a pyramidal, loose, open habit; height to 50 feet (15 m) in the landscape. A wide selection of cultivars offers variety in shape, size, and color. Zones 4–8.
WHEN TO PRUNE: In spring.
HOW TO PRUNE: There's little work to do with the plants in this genus! If the plant you're working with has a central leader at all, prune to retain it. Otherwise, simply use thinning cuts to remove the occasional misplaced branch.

Cornus spp.　　　　　　Cornaceae

DOGWOODS

Fall is a good time to prune dogwoods to minimize the spread of diseases and to avoid "bleeding" sap. Remove watersprouts and crossing or rubbing limbs.

DESCRIPTION: Dogwoods are among the most well-known small deciduous trees. They grow to about 25 feet (7.5 m), often with trunks branching close to the ground. Give dogwoods good drainage, mulch, partial shade, and moist, humus-rich soil.
　　C. florida (flowering dogwood): Has a horizontally layered growth habit; height to 40 feet (12 m) under favorable conditions. Showy white bracts surround true flowers in early spring before the leaves; red berries follow in fall. Zones 5–8.
　　C. kousa (kousa dogwood): Has a more vase-shaped form without the strong horizontal character of flowering dogwood; height to 20 feet (6 m). White, star-like, pointed bracts appear later in the spring after the leaves have emerged, followed by raspberry-like fruits. Peeling bark leaves mottled patches of browns and tans. Kousa dogwood tolerates the sun and drought conditions that can decimate flowering dogwood. Zones 5–7.
WHEN TO PRUNE: In fall. Avoid spring pruning to reduce the spread of anthracnose in flowering dogwood; also, dogwoods tend to "bleed" sap when pruned in the spring.
HOW TO PRUNE: Dogwoods naturally develop a beautiful form without much pruning. Simply cut out crossing or rubbing limbs. Also prune out any watersprouts; these strong, upright shoots can ruin the plant's form.

Cotinus spp.   Anacardiaceae

SMOKE TREES

Smoke trees produce showy seed heads and often have dramatic fall color as well. Prune in late winter or early spring to thin out long stems and to encourage branching.

DESCRIPTION: Smoke trees are named for their finely textured flowers that appear in late spring or early summer. Fuzzy fruits carry on the flowers' billowy appearance well after flowering. Smoke trees grow best in full sun and well-drained soil.

    C. coggygria (smoke tree): Large shrub or small tree; height to 15 feet (4.5 m). Blue-green foliage turns to purple, red, or yellow in the fall, though not reliably in the South. 'Royal Purple' has purplish leaves, flowers, and fruit. Zones 4–8.

    C. obovatus (American smoke tree): Medium-sized tree; height to 30 feet (9 m). Though not common in the retail trade, this North American native is well worth the effort to obtain; it has all of the features of *C. coggygria* and even more remarkable fall color. Zones 3–8.

WHEN TO PRUNE: In late winter or early spring.

HOW TO PRUNE: The shrubbier *C. coggygria* benefits from occasional pruning; head back long shoots to encourage branching. You may also want to use thinning cuts to limit its size. Train American smoke tree to a single leader as you would most shade trees. Thin occasionally to reduce wind resistance in the crown.

SPECIAL TIPS: If you're growing a purple-leaved type for its foliage, consider cutting the stems to a few inches (cm) above the ground each year. The new shoots will produce larger, showier leaves (but no flowers).

Crataegus spp.   Rosaceae

HAWTHORNS

Hawthorns often produce thorny side branches near the ground. Prune off a few of the lowest branches in late winter each year to make it easier to walk or work underneath.

DESCRIPTION: Hawthorns are thorny, deciduous, flowering trees with single or multiple trunks. The white flowers appear in midspring and are followed by reddish fruits in the fall and—in a good year—remarkable fall color. They require full sun and good drainage.

    C. crus-galli (cockspur hawthorn): Has a broad, rounded, horizontally layered outline and purplish bronze fall color; height to 30 feet (9 m). 'Inermis' lacks thorns. Zones 4–7.

    C. phaenopyrum (Washington hawthorn): Grows in a broadly oval form; height to 25 feet (7.5 m). Fall color can be orange, purple, or scarlet. Zones 4–8.

    C. viridis (green hawthorn): Sports fall colors in purples and reds; height to 25 feet (7.5 m). 'Winter King' is well known for the brightness and persistence of its red berries. Zones 4–7.

WHEN TO PRUNE: In late winter.

HOW TO PRUNE: Train young hawthorns to a central leader. Remove lower branches as the trees grow to protect passersby from the thorns (or plant a thornless cultivar). Remove sucker growth and crossing limbs.

SPECIAL TIPS: See the Hawthorns entry on page 37 for tips on using hawthorns for a hedge.

Fagus spp.   Fagaceae

BEECHES

Beeches grow slowly to form large trees. Prune young trees in summer or early fall to encourage strong branch angles. Remove lower branches if you need room to walk under the tree.

DESCRIPTION: Beeches are deciduous, spreading trees with impressive stature for large landscapes. They have beautiful, smooth gray bark that often becomes wrinkled with age, looking like an elephant's hide. Beeches prosper in full sun and well-drained, moist soil. They are sensitive to soil compaction and other kinds of root disturbance.

> *F. grandifolia* (American beech): Glossy dark green leaves edged with sharp teeth. Height 50–70 feet (15–21 m). Zones 4–8.

> *F. sylvatica* (European beech): Glossy dark green leaves with wavy edges. Height to about 60 feet (18 m). Zones 5–7.

WHEN TO PRUNE: In summer or early fall.

HOW TO PRUNE: Train young beeches to a central leader. Remove any branches that join the trunk at a narrow angle; they are prone to breaking when the tree is old and carrying a lot of weight. Lower limbs, when left unpruned, tend to sweep the ground and—especially on European beeches—create a "room" beneath the tree. Some very old beeches have even been known to root at the tips of those descending branches, creating a ring of trees around the original one. If you don't want lower branches sweeping the ground, remove them gradually over several years as the tree matures.

SPECIAL TIPS: Beech is a remarkably hard-wooded species. Be sure your pruning tools are sharp!

Fraxinus spp.   Oleaceae

ASHES

Ashes grow fairly quickly to form handsome shade trees. Good pruning and training when an ash tree is young will encourage a strong main trunk and sturdy side branches.

DESCRIPTION: These deciduous shade trees can grow 60–70 feet (18–21 m) tall. They are remarkably tolerant of urban sites and other challenging growing conditions. They prefer full sun and even moisture. Because the species reseed readily, seedless cultivars are a good choice for lower maintenance.

> *F. americana* (white ash): Has a broad, spreading, rounded crown. Fall colors include yellow, rose, and a hazy purple. Zones 4–9. 'Autumn Purple' is a popular seedless cultivar hardy to Zone 5.

> *F. pennsylvanica* (green ash): Has a slightly more upright and less spreading form than white ash. Fall foliage is yellow. Zones 2–9. The cultivar 'Marshall's Seedless' grows in Zones 3–7.

WHEN TO PRUNE: In fall.

HOW TO PRUNE: Train young trees to a single central leader. Because of the opposite branching habit, these trees tend to form twin leaders, a structural weakness that is prone to breakage as the tree ages. If you spot competing leaders on a young tree, prune one out.

Ginkgo biloba   Ginkgoaceae

GINKGO

Easy-care ginkgo trees rarely need much pruning. Simply prune young trees to a sturdy central trunk, and remove lower branches gradually if you need room to walk underneath.

DESCRIPTION: Ginkgo, also known as maidenhair tree, is a single-trunked tree that is upright or rounded in youth and broadly rounded when mature. The fan-shaped leaves turn yellow in fall and all seem to drop on the same day. On female trees, fall color is accompanied by round, 1-inch (2.5 cm) fruits that are tan to orange with a white, waxy bloom. The fruits contain butyric acid (which makes a rancid butter smell) and have a powerfully bad odor; their inner kernel is a delicacy in certain Asian cultures. Most nurseries now only sell male trees, but always ask before you buy if you don't want the fruits. Ginkgos require full sun and good drainage; they tolerate urban conditions well. Zones 4–7.

WHEN TO PRUNE: In spring.

HOW TO PRUNE: Prune young trees to a central leader. They need little else except for an occasional limbing up (removal of lower branches) to allow room for people to walk underneath. Do this gradually over several years as the tree matures.

Gleditsia triacanthos   Leguminosae

HONEY LOCUST

Honey locusts often form sprouts on their trunks. Prune in late summer or fall to remove those sprouts, as well as any crossing, rubbing, or awkwardly placed branches.

DESCRIPTION: This deciduous shade tree has a vase-shaped habit and an open crown. The finely tex-tured compound leaves give an airy feeling and cast a light shade on the ground below. Fall color is yellow. Fall cleanup is remarkably easy because the small leaflets either blow away or work their way down into the grass or groundcover below; they don't mat down on the lawn. Inconspicuous flow-ers are followed by strap-like brown seedpods on all but the seedless cultivars (like 'Shademaster'). Thorns stout enough to go through boot soles grow on trunks and limbs; a thornless cultivar like 'Moraine' is the best choice for most landscapes. Honey locusts perform best in full sun and well-drained soil. 'Sunburst' features golden yellow foliage as it emerges in the spring and throughout the summer at the branch tips. Zones 4–9.

WHEN TO PRUNE: In late summer into fall.

HOW TO PRUNE: Prune for a strong central leader on a young tree. If you'll need to walk or mow under the tree, gradually remove lower branches over a period of several years. Remove crossing, rubbing, or errant branches as well as the occasional trunk sprouts that emerge during summer.

| *Hamamelis* spp.　　　　　Hamamelidaceae | *Ilex* spp.　　　　　Aquifoliaceae |

WITCH HAZELS

HOLLIES

Witch hazels usually look best with little or no pruning. Shrubby types may produce many suckers; remove these suckers as needed to keep plants in their allotted space.

Pinching or shearing the tips of young holly trees in late spring will encourage compact growth and maintain the plants' natural pyramidal form.

DESCRIPTION: Witch hazels are deciduous, large shrubs or small trees that bloom in the fall, winter, or spring. The fragrant flowers tend to be long-lasting because the petals unroll in favorable weather but can roll back up if there is a freeze. Seed capsules follow the flowers. Fall color tends to be a dull yellow. Witch hazels prefer partial shade and humus-rich soil.

H. x *intermedia* (witch hazel): Height 15 to 20 feet (4.5–6 m). Vigorous plants that train readily into tree forms. Flowers may be yellow, orange-red, or reddish, depending on the cultivar. Zones 5–8.

H. mollis (Chinese witch hazel): Height 10–15 feet (3–4.5 m). Sulfur yellow or yellow-red flowers unroll in midwinter. Zones 5–8.

H. vernalis (vernal witch hazel): Height 6–10 feet (1.8–3 m). Blooms in late winter to early spring. Zones 4–8.

H. virginiana (common witch hazel): Height 10–15 feet (3–4.5 m). Blooms in the fall as the leaves are dropping. Zones 4–8.

WHEN TO PRUNE: After flowering.

HOW TO PRUNE: Witch hazels need little pruning, except for the removal of the occasional awkward branch. Rejuvenate an overgrown shrub form by removing one-third of the oldest growth close to the ground each year.

DESCRIPTION: Tree hollies are typically pyramidal in form, with spiny, evergreen leaves and red, yellow, or orange berries in the fall. Hollies are dioecious, so you'll need to grow both male and female plants for berry production. They prefer partial shade, protection from wind, and moist, well-drained, humus-rich soil.

I. aquifolium (English holly): Grows tall in its native lands but rarely grows taller than 20 feet (6 m) in American landscapes. Best in Zones 6–7.

I. x *attenuata* (Topel holly): Height 20–30 feet (6–9 m). Narrowly conical in form, finely textured, and well berried in most years. Outstanding cultivars include 'Foster #2' (Foster's holly) and 'Savannah'; mostly in Zones 6–9.

I. opaca (American holly): Pyramidal in youth and maturing to a more open form; height 15–30 feet (4.5–9 m). The foliage tends to be a medium green, sometimes dull. Red berries appear on the current season's growth. Zones 5–9.

WHEN TO PRUNE: In late spring.

HOW TO PRUNE: To encourage compact growth, pinch or shear the tips of young trees, following the natural pyramidal shape. Resist the temptation to keep shearing once the tree has filled in and is growing well, unless your goal is a formal look.

SPECIAL TIPS: See the Hollies entry on page 41 to learn about the shrubbier hollies.

WALNUTS

GOLDEN-RAIN TREE

Give walnut trees lots of room and they'll seldom need much pruning. Trim off lower branches gradually if you need room to walk or work underneath.

Golden-rain tree forms a dense, rounded crown with many large clusters of yellow flowers in summer. Prune in late winter or early spring to remove dead, damaged, or crossing branches.

DESCRIPTION: Walnuts are deciduous trees that perform best in full sun and deep, moist, well-drained soil. They provide shade and edible nuts. In the garden and landscape, walnuts can have an inhibiting effect on other plants. Use them in large-scale situations where they can be planted alone or grouped with other walnuts.

J. nigra (black walnut): Has a clear, straight trunk and an upright oval crown; height 50–75 feet (15–22.5 m). Seeds cloaked in thick green husks form and begin to drop in the fall. Zones 5–7.

J. regia (English walnut, Persian walnut): Height 40–60 feet (12–18 m). Similar to black walnut but more squat and rounded in outline. Zones 6–8. The Carpathian walnut is a selection that is useful to Zone 5.

WHEN TO PRUNE: In fall.

HOW TO PRUNE: Prune young trees to a central leader. If you need to be able to walk beneath the tree, remove lower branches gradually over several years to allow for headroom. Remove crossing or rubbing branches. Mature trees need little pruning unless they have been neglected; if so, call a reputable tree service to do the work.

SPECIAL TIPS: For further information on growing walnuts for nut production, see the Walnut entry on page 131.

DESCRIPTION: This single-trunked deciduous tree forms a dense, rounded crown 30–40 feet high (9–12 m) with an equal or greater spread. Yellow flowers appear at the branch tips in July. The fruits that follow begin green, turn pink, and then turn brown, looking like many brown paper bags. The pinnately compound leaves turn yellow in fall. Golden-rain tree appreciates full sun and well-drained soil. It is highly adaptable and tolerates urban conditions well. Zones 5–9.

WHEN TO PRUNE: In late winter or early spring before growth begins.

HOW TO PRUNE: Train young trees to a central leader. Remove lower limbs gradually over several years if you need room to walk under the tree. Remove crossing or rubbing branches, as well as those that are broken or dying back.

CRAPE MYRTLE

On tree-form crape myrtles, gradually remove the lower branches to expose the beautifully mottled bark. Also prune out suckers, watersprouts, and crossing or rubbing branches.

DESCRIPTION: Crape myrtle is a deciduous tree or shrub that grows to 20 feet (6 m) with a single or multistemmed trunk. The form is normally upright and narrowly vase-shaped. Some cultivars have attractive, peeling bark, giving the tree a sculptural appearance. White, pink, or carmine flowers bloom in the summer on the current season's wood. Fall color varies with the cultivar and weather conditions, but it can be outstanding. Best in full sun and good drainage. Zones 7–9. North of Zone 7, crape myrtles are often grown as shrubs or perennials.

WHEN TO PRUNE: In late winter or early spring before growth begins or in summer after flowering.

HOW TO PRUNE: Shape tree forms by removing sucker shoots, watersprouts, and crossing or rubbing limbs. Remove lower limbs gradually over time to expose the bark. After bloom, remove the spent flowers and seed heads to promote abundant flowering in the future. If the stems die back in winter in your climate, cut them back to the ground before growth begins in spring.

SPECIAL TIPS: In the long growing seasons of Zones 8–9, the midsummer removal of spent blooms may bring on extra flowers in fall.

LARCHES

Young larches have a naturally graceful, pyramidal habit that needs little pruning. If the central leader (tip shoot) is damaged, train another to keep the plant growing upright.

DESCRIPTION: Larches are tall, single-trunked trees. Unlike most needle-leaved conifers, larches are deciduous; their needles turn yellow and drop to the ground each fall. They prefer sunny sites with moist, acid, humus-rich soil in mostly northern climates.

L. decidua (European larch): Has a pyramidal form; height 70–100 feet (21–30 m). Horizontal branches from the trunk bear pendant branchlets. Zones 3–6.

L. laricina (tamarack): Similar in appearance to European larch, though smaller; height 40–80 feet (12–24 m). Zones 2–4.

WHEN TO PRUNE: In late winter or early spring before growth begins or in summer.

HOW TO PRUNE: Larches need minimal maintenance. Prune to keep the central leader—its loss can cause the graceful, pyramidal habit to revert to a bushy form. See the Firs entry on page 62 in this chapter to find out how to retrain a new leader. Needs little else.

Liquidambar styraciflua   Hamamelidaceae

SWEET GUM

Sweet gums grow to be large shade trees, so give them plenty of room. Prune, if necessary, in late winter or early spring to remove crossing branches and to promote a sturdy main trunk.

DESCRIPTION: Sweet gum is a deciduous shade tree. Pyramidal when young, it matures to an upright oval form to 60–120 feet (18–36 m) high. The inconspicuous flowers are followed by hard-beaked, round, 1-inch (2.5 cm) capsules in fall. The star-shaped leaves turn to reds and oranges in fall. Sweet gum grows best in full sun and in soil with steady moisture and good drainage. Zones 5–8.

WHEN TO PRUNE: In late winter or early spring before growth begins.

HOW TO PRUNE: Sweet gum needs little pruning. Train young trees to a central leader. Prune out crossing or misplaced limbs. Remove lower limbs gradually over several years if you need room to walk or mow around the base of the tree.

SPECIAL TIPS: The hard seed capsules can be a problem in home landscapes, as they are unpleasant to walk on and break down very slowly. Consider growing 'Rotundiloba', a seedless selection with leaves that have rounded lobes.

Liriodendron tulipifera   Magnoliaceae

TULIP TREE

Train young tulip trees to a single center trunk with sturdy, wide-angled branches. During the dormant season, prune as needed to remove crossing or rubbing limbs.

DESCRIPTION: Deciduous tulip trees have an upright form with a straight trunk that can grow 70–90 feet (21–27 m) high. Tulip-like flowers with yellow-green petals and an orange base bloom high in the branches shortly after the leaves open. Often, if the tree is quite tall, the petals that have fallen to the ground are the only evidence of flowering. Later in the season, winged fruits form where the flowers were. The leaves turn yellow in fall before dropping. Tulip tree grows best in full sun and deep, moist, loamy soil. Zones 5–8.

WHEN TO PRUNE: In the dormant season.

HOW TO PRUNE: Train newly planted trees to a central leader. If you need room to walk near the base of the tree, gradually remove lower limbs over the first several years. Remove crossing or rubbing branches.

Magnolia spp. Magnoliaceae   *Malus* spp. Rosaceae

MAGNOLIAS

CRAB APPLES

Prune magnolias after flowering to eliminate dead, crossing, or rubbing branches. If you have the room, leave the lower branches; otherwise, remove them gradually.

Crab apples require considerably more pruning than most landscape trees. Remove suckers and watersprouts regularly, and thin crowded growth to keep the center open to sunlight and air.

DESCRIPTION: Magnolias are evergreen or deciduous single- or multiple-trunked trees or shrubs. They are popular for their dramatic spring flowers, beautiful summer foliage, showy seeds, and attractive bark. They prefer full sun and evenly moist soil.

M. grandiflora (southern magnolia): Evergreen with glossy green, leathery leaves. Tends to be pyramidal; height to 75 feet (22.5 m). Waxy, white, fragrant flowers abound in late spring, followed by sporadic blooming throughout the summer. Seedpods open in fall to reveal bright red seeds. Tolerates wet soil. Zones 6–9.

M. x *soulangiana* (saucer magnolia): Multiple-stemmed deciduous shrub or tree; height to about 25 feet (7.5 m). Pink or magenta flowers appear before the leaves in spring and are sometimes lost to spring frosts. Zones 5–8.

M. virginiana (sweet bay magnolia): Semi-evergreen, single- or multiple-stemmed tree with a loose, open habit; height to about 40 feet (12 m). Fragrant, waxy, white flowers bloom in the spring and are followed by showy seedpods. Tolerates wet soil. Zones 6–9.

WHEN TO PRUNE: After flowering.

HOW TO PRUNE: Train southern and sweet bay magnolia to a central leader and remove crossing limbs. Saucer magnolia, when grown as a shrub, may benefit from the occasional removal of old growth at ground level.

DESCRIPTION: Crab apples are deciduous trees or shrubs popular for their beautiful spring flowers and showy fruits. There are countless cultivars available; many have resulted from breeding programs aimed at disease-resistance. Form, character, flower, fruit, and fall color all vary with the cultivar; most grow in Zones 4–7. Plant in full sun and evenly moist, well-drained soil.

WHEN TO PRUNE: In late winter or early spring before growth begins or in late spring following bloom.

HOW TO PRUNE: Crab apples require considerably more pruning than most of the tree species listed here, even the big shade trees. Train young trees to a central leader. Remove any branches that are dead, dying, crossing, or rubbing to allow better air flow and sunlight to the interior of the tree; this will discourage fungal diseases, reduce the wind resistance that can cause breakage, and promote abundant flowering. Also remove the sucker shoots and watersprouts that emerge regularly. If the tree has been neglected, spread the trimming out over a period of several years. Otherwise, the tree will respond to heavy pruning by producing a big crop of watersprouts.

SPECIAL TIPS: Fire blight can be a problem during a wet spring. For tips on spotting the symptoms and pruning accordingly, see "Protect Pears from Fire Blight" on page 109.

Nyssa sylvatica   Nyssaceae

BLACK TUPELO

Black tupelo is a handsome shade tree that needs little annual care. Prune in fall, if needed, to remove dead, damaged, or crossing branches and those that are too close to the ground.

DESCRIPTION: Black tupelo, also known as black gum or sour gum, is a deciduous, upright, pyramidal tree with distinctly horizontal lateral branches. It can grow 40–80 feet (12–24 m) high. The inconspicuous flowers are followed by black fruits. Sour gum is known and grown for its spectacular red, burgundy, and orange fall color. It prospers in sun to semishade and acid soil. Although it tolerates wet soil, it performs well in soil with good drainage and even moisture. Zones 4–9.

WHEN TO PRUNE: In fall.

HOW TO PRUNE: Needs little pruning. Train young trees to a central leader. Remove any crossing or rubbing limbs. Prune off lower limbs gradually over several years if you need room to walk or mow around the base of the tree.

Oxydendrum arboreum   Ericaceae

SOURWOOD

Sourwood is a slow-growing, medium-sized tree grown for its white flowers and showy fall color. If possible, allow room for the lower branches; otherwise, remove them gradually.

DESCRIPTION: Sourwood has a pyramidal form when young, becoming rounded at the top with drooping branches. It grows to a height of 25–30 feet (7.5–9 m). Cascading white flowers resembling the blooms of lily-of-the-valley open in June and July. In fall, the leaves turn a brilliant red before dropping. Sourwood grows best in full sun to partial shade and in moist, humus-rich soil. Zones 5–9.

WHEN TO PRUNE: In summer after flowering.

HOW TO PRUNE: Needs little pruning. Remove crossing or rubbing limbs. Prune off lower limbs gradually if you need room to walk or mow around the base of the tree.

Picea spp.   Pinaceae

SPRUCES

Allow plenty of room for young spruces to reach their mature size and your pruning chores will be minimal. If necessary, pinch part of the new shoots in spring to encourage compact growth.

DESCRIPTION: Spruces are needle-leaved evergreens with a naturally pyramidal form. Give spruces plenty of room: They can grow very quickly to 30–60 feet (9–18 m), depending on the conditions and species. Spruces grow best in cool climates with full sun and moist, well-drained soil.

P. abies (Norway spruce): Has horizontal limbs with pendant branchlets. Zones 2–6.

P. glauca (white spruce): Has a narrow, pyramidal form and becomes spire-like with age and optimum growing conditions. The cultivar 'Conica' is the popular dwarf Alberta spruce; 'Densata' is the tough Black Hills spruce. Zones 2–6.

P. omorika (Serbian spruce): Distinguished by the white undersides of its needles, revealed by the graceful upward arc of the branches. Zones 4–6.

P. pungens (Colorado spruce): Has a stiffly pyramidal form. The various blue spruce cultivars are in this species, including 'Koster'. Zones 2–6.

WHEN TO PRUNE: In spring, when the new growth (called "candles") is half developed.

HOW TO PRUNE: To encourage an open or scrawny spruce to fill in, pinch off one-half to two-thirds of each candle. This causes more buds to break behind the branch tip. Be sure to preserve the central leader, otherwise your spruce will turn into a big, fat bush. See the Firs entry on page 62 for tips on how to replace a lost leader.

Pinus spp.   Pinaceae

PINES

Keep pine trees growing upright by retraining a new leader (tip shoot) if the original one gets broken or damaged. Pinch new shoots, if needed, to promote bushy growth.

DESCRIPTION: These needle-leaved evergreens tend to be pyramidal in youth and flat-topped at maturity when given plenty of room. They prefer full sun and well-drained soil.

P. nigra (Austrian pine): Develops into a picturesque, flat-topped tree with massive limbs and trunk; height 50–60 feet (15–30 m). The bark on older trees becomes gray-white with deep black fissures. Zones 4–6.

P. strobus (eastern white pine): Graceful tree with long, flexible needles; height 60–80 feet (18–24 m). Zones 3–6.

P. sylvestris (Scotch pine): Has a stiffer appearance due to its short, stiff, blue-green needles. Peeling bark reveals an orange inner bark in the upper trunk and limbs. Height 30–60 feet (9–18 m). Zones 2–6.

WHEN TO PRUNE: In spring, when the new growth is at the "candle" stage.

HOW TO PRUNE: To make an open tree more full, pinch off half of each candle. Be sure that the terminal leader stays intact, as its loss means that your tree will become a bush. See the Firs entry on page 62 for tips on how to replace a lost leader.

SPECIAL TIPS: Shearing is the common method of pruning pines for Christmas tree production. If you like the formal look, shearing is an option.

Platanus spp.   Platanaceae

SYCAMORES

Give sycamores lots of room and good training when they are young; they'll grow quickly into large shade trees. Prune in late winter or early spring to promote sturdy branches.

DESCRIPTION: With peeling bark revealing white, tan, and green patches, this massive tree makes a stunning impact. Sycamores, also called plane-trees, have broad, spreading crowns 50–90 feet (15–27 m) high. One-inch (2.5 cm) seed balls appear and drop late in the season. The seed balls, shedding bark, and large deciduous leaves may pose a maintenance problem in small yards; syca-mores are better planted in large-scale landscapes. They perform best with full sun, steady moisture, and lots of space. In nature, they grow in wet areas and thrive in landscapes that are similarly wet. Zones 5–8.

WHEN TO PRUNE: In late winter or early spring before growth begins.

HOW TO PRUNE: Train young trees to a central leader, removing lower limbs gradually over several years if you need room for people and their activities. Remove crossing or rubbing limbs as well as branches that join the trunk at a narrow angle.

Prunus spp.   Rosaceae

FLOWERING CHERRIES

Flowering cherries generally don't need much pruning to keep them looking their best. Trim as needed after flowering to remove dead, damaged, crossing, or rubbing branches.

DESCRIPTION: All of the cherries are deciduous and appreciate full sun and well-drained soil. They are widely grown for their beautiful spring flowers; some species also have showy bark.
  P. cerasifera (Myrobalan plum): Upright tree; height 15–20 feet (4.5–6 m). Pink flowers appear in early spring before the leaves. The cultivar 'Atropurpurea' is the popular purple-leaved plum. Zones 4–8.
  P. serrulata (Japanese flowering cherry): Vase-shaped tree; height 20–25 feet (6–7.5 m). Single or double, white or pink flowers bloom in early spring. 'Kwanzan' is a popular double-flowered cultivar. Zones 5–7.
  P. subhirtella (Higan cherry): Full, round-headed tree; height to 25 feet (7.5 m). The pale to deep pink, single or double flowers bloom before the leaves appear. Can have outstanding fall color. 'Pendula' is a popular weeping cultivar. Zones 5–9.

WHEN TO PRUNE: After flowering.

HOW TO PRUNE: Remove crossing or rubbing limbs. On the nonweeping forms, you may choose to gradually remove lower limbs over several years to allow room for walking or mowing.

SPECIAL TIPS: Weeping cherries occasionally revert back to their original upright form. Remove any upright branches that appear or eventually you'll have an entirely upright tree.

Pyrus calleryana	Rosaceae	*Quercus* spp.	Fagaceae

CALLERY PEAR

Callery pears benefit from especially careful pruning and training. Remove branches that join the trunk at a narrow angle, and thin out multiple branches that emerge from one spot.

DESCRIPTION: Pyramidal in youth, these deciduous upright trees eventually develop a round, full head 25–40 feet (7.5–12 m) high. White flowers bloom in spring before the leaves appear. Brilliant red and orange fall foliage is accompanied by persistent, hard, round fruits. Callery pear grows best in full sun and well-drained soil.

'Bradford' is a popular cultivar that has become problematic because of its form: Narrow branch angles and closely crowded limbs result in structural weakness. Crowded branches increase wind resistance and surface area on which ice and snow accumulate. Branches then split away at the base, disfiguring the tree and leaving gaping wounds. When buying, look for improved cultivars such as 'Aristocrat' or 'Cleveland Select'. Zones 5–8.

WHEN TO PRUNE: In late winter or early spring before growth begins or in spring after flowering.

HOW TO PRUNE: Train young trees to a central leader and for even distribution of limbs along the trunk; if you see two limbs growing side by side, from essentially the same point, remove one. Prune out branches that join the trunk at a narrow angle (less than 45 degrees). Also remove any crossing, rubbing, or inwardly growing limbs. If you need room to walk or mow around the base of the tree, gradually remove lower limbs over several years.

OAKS

Prune young oaks in late winter or early spring to remove crossing or rubbing branches and to encourage a strong main trunk. Mature oaks seldom need any pruning.

DESCRIPTION: Oaks are large, broadly spreading, deciduous or evergreen trees. These sturdy shade trees can reach heights of 60–80 feet (18–24 m). They grow best in full sun with plenty of room and well-drained soil.

Q. alba (white oak): Has distinctive ash-gray, layered bark; height 60–80 feet (1.8–2.4 m). Fall color on the deeply lobed deciduous leaves is often a soft pink-burgundy. Zones 3–8.

Q. palustris (pin oak): Pyramidal when young; upright, open, and irregular with age; height 60–70 feet (1.8–2.1 m). On limestone or alkaline soil, the deciduous foliage can become yellow with iron chlorosis. Zones 5–8.

Q. phellos (willow oak): Has narrow, willow-like deciduous leaves that give it a fine-textured appearance. Zones 6–9.

Q. rubra (northern red oak): Known for its impressive, large-scale presence and its red fall color; height 60–70 feet (1.8–2.1 m). Zones 4–8.

WHEN TO PRUNE: In late winter or early spring before growth begins. In areas where oak wilt is a problem, prune only in dry weather.

HOW TO PRUNE: Because oaks have naturally stable architecture and very strong wood, they require very little pruning. Train young trees to a central leader; remove any crossing or rubbing branches.

WILLOWS

JAPANESE PAGODA TREE

Prune willows in late summer to remove dead, damaged, crossing, or rubbing branches. Trim weeping forms as needed to keep the branch tips from trailing on the ground.

DESCRIPTION: These deciduous, narrow-leaved trees tend to be weak-wooded, prone to breakage, and short-lived. Willows perform best in sunny, moist, large-scale locations where the litter from falling twigs isn't a real maintenance problem.

S. alba (white willow): Upright tree; height to 75 feet (22.5 m). The slender, pliant branches turn a vibrant yellow as sap begins to rise in spring. 'Tristis' is one popular weeping cultivar. Zones 2–8.

S. matsudana (Pekin willow): Height to 40 feet (12 m). The cultivar 'Tortuosa' is the interesting corkscrew willow. Zones 5–8.

WHEN TO PRUNE: In late summer.

HOW TO PRUNE: Stake young trees of the weeping forms to keep them from bending too soon. Be prepared to remove dead wood as it appears and to trim weeping branches so they don't drag on the ground.

SPECIAL TIPS: Willows can also grow in shrubby forms. Some species—including *S. caprea* and *S. melanostachys*—are commonly called "pussy willow" for their silky spring catkins. On these, prune out a third of the oldest stems to the ground after flowering each year. Other willows, such as *S. alba* 'Britzensis', produce colorful stems. Keep these forms vigorous by cutting all the stems to a few inches (cm) above the ground in late winter or early spring.

Japanese scholar tree tends to grow in a rather loose, open form, especially for the first few years. Prune young trees in fall for shape and to encourage a strong main trunk.

DESCRIPTION: Pyramidal in youth and broadly rounded at maturity, Japanese pagoda tree—also called Chinese scholar tree—can grow to 75 feet (22.5 m). The pinnately compound leaves have small leaflets, giving the tree a fine-textured appearance. The dark green foliage makes an excellent background for the fragrant white flowers that bloom in July and August. In fall, pendant green seedpods that look like strings of green pearls appear; the leaves remain green until they drop. Known for its tolerance of challenging urban environments, Japanese pagoda tree grows best in full sun and well-drained soil. Zones 4–7.

WHEN TO PRUNE: In fall.

HOW TO PRUNE: Train young trees to a central leader and remove any crossing or rubbing branches. If you need room to walk beneath the tree, gradually remove lower limbs over several years.

Sorbus spp.   Rosaceae

MOUNTAIN ASHES

Mountain ashes are planted for their showy white flowers and colorful fall fruit. If fire blight turns branch tips brown or black, prune damaged tips back into healthy wood.

DESCRIPTION: Mountain ashes are small- to medium-sized deciduous trees that produce clusters of white flowers in late spring followed by red-orange berries in fall. They prefer full sun and well-drained soil.

    S. alnifolia (Korean mountain ash): Has simple leaves and is less susceptible to the insects and diseases that so often plague this genus; height 40–50 feet (12–15 m). Zones 4–6.

    S. americana (American mountain ash): Has compound leaves; height to 30 feet (9 m). Useful for native or wildlife plantings. Zones 2–6.

    S. aucuparia (European mountain ash): Also has compound leaves; height 20–40 feet (6–12 m). Though this is the most commonly planted mountain ash, its susceptibility to fire blight, borers, and tent caterpillars limits its use. Zones 3–6.

WHEN TO PRUNE: In late winter or early spring before growth begins.

HOW TO PRUNE: Train young trees to a central leader and remove crossing or rubbing branches. Where head clearance is necessary, remove lower limbs gradually over several years.

SPECIAL TIPS: See "Protect Pears from Fire Blight" on page 109 for tips on identifying and pruning out fire blight damage.

Taxodium distichum   Taxodiaceae

BALD CYPRESS

Bald cypress doesn't demand much regular attention. Prune as needed during the dormant season to remove crossing or rubbing limbs and any lower branches that are in the way.

DESCRIPTION: Pyramidal when young, bald cypress matures to a more irregular form 50–70 feet (15–21 m) high. The compound needles on this deciduous conifer turn to an orange-brown before dropping in fall. Globular cones appear in mid-summer. With age, the bark becomes stringy and fibrous and root flares at the base of the trunk develop into buttresses. On trees growing in or around water, wooden "knees" rise from the roots out of the moist soil or water. Bald cypresses grow best in full sun and moist soil; however, they don't require the wet conditions found in their native habitats. Zones 5–9.

WHEN TO PRUNE: During the dormant season.

HOW TO PRUNE: Train young trees to a central leader. If you need room to walk or mow beneath the tree, remove lower limbs gradually over several years. Remove any crossing or rubbing limbs as well.

TAXODIUM 81

Tilia spp.   Tiliaceae   *Tsuga* spp.   Pinaceae

LINDENS   # HEMLOCKS

Train young lindens carefully to encourage strong branch angles. Thin out multiple branches that emerge from the same point on the trunk. Remove suckers as they appear.

Hemlocks need little pruning when allowed to grow in their graceful natural form. Simply trim out dead, damaged, or poorly placed shoots in spring or summer.

DESCRIPTION: Pyramidal in youth, lindens often become round-headed with age. They can reach 50–80 feet (15–24 m) tall. Fragrant flowers that are attractive to honeybees dangle from leafy bracts in early summer. By fall the flowers have developed into small, round fruits. The heart-shaped leaves turn yellow before dropping. Plant lindens in full sun and well-drained soil.

T. americana (basswood, American linden): Grows into a huge tree with a round head; height 60–80 feet (18–24 m). Zones 2–7.

T. cordata (little-leaved linden): Smaller and tends to keep its pyramidal shape; height 30–40 feet (9–12 m). Zones 3–7.

T. tomentosa (silver linden): Distinguished by the silvery undersides of its leaves; height 50–70 feet (15–21 m). Zones 5–7.

WHEN TO PRUNE: In late winter or early spring before growth begins.

HOW TO PRUNE: Lindens naturally produce numerous sucker shoots at their base; be prepared to remove them periodically. Train young trees to a central leader. Little-leaved lindens exhibit some of the same structural flaws as 'Bradford' pear (see the Callery pear entry on page 79 for details). Look for multiple limbs that originate from the same point on the trunk and remove all but one.

DESCRIPTION: Hemlocks are graceful, needle-leaved evergreens with a loosely pyramidal form and a soft texture. The tip of the tree often nods away from prevailing winds. Hemlocks prefer cool climates and moist, humus-rich, well-drained soil. Do not plant them where they will be exposed to high winds, salt, or pollution.

T. canadensis (Canada hemlock, eastern hemlock): Height to 75 feet (22.5 m), although 30 feet (9 m) is more likely in the landscape. Zones 3–8.

T. caroliniana (Carolina hemlock): Has blunter needles and generally a deeper green color; height to about 75 feet (22.5 m). Zones 5–7.

WHEN TO PRUNE: In spring or summer.

HOW TO PRUNE: Needs little pruning when grown as a tree, singly or in groups. Shear if you desire a more formal look.

SPECIAL TIPS: See the Hemlocks entry on page 52 for tips on using these trees as a hedge.

ELMS

JAPANESE ZELKOVA

Prune young elms in late winter or early spring to remove dead, injured, crossing, or rubbing branches. Gradually remove lower limbs if you need room to walk or work under the tree.

DESCRIPTION: Elms are deciduous shade trees that prefer full sun and well-drained soil.

U. americana (American elm, white elm): Known for its broadly vase-shaped form that has provided great canopies over many American streets; height to almost 100 feet (30 m). Dutch elm disease (DED), aided by the elm bark beetle, has decimated much of the urban population of American elms. The species is rarely planted, except for the newly bred DED-resistant cultivars that are being tested. Zones 2–8.

U. parvifolia (Chinese elm, lacebark elm): Broad-spreading tree; height 40–50 feet (12–15 m). Noted for the dramatic effect of its bark, which flakes off to reveal patches of tan, green, and cream. Yellow or purplish fall color. It is resistant to DED. Zones 5–8.

U. pumila (Siberian elm): Sometimes incorrectly sold as Chinese elm. Mentioned here only to warn readers away from it. Notoriously weak-wooded, this species quickly becomes massive and essentially collapses under its own weight. Zones 3–8.

WHEN TO PRUNE: In late winter or early spring before growth begins.

HOW TO PRUNE: Train young trees to a central leader. Gradually remove lower limbs over several years if you need room to walk or mow under the tree. Also remove crossing, rubbing, and dead wood.

Japanese zelkova seldom needs pruning. Trim as needed in late summer or fall to thin out dense growth and to remove dead wood and crossing or rubbing limbs.

DESCRIPTION: This deciduous, vase-shaped elm relative has been suggested as one possible substitute for the beloved but disease-prone American elm. Japanese zelkova grows to about 80 feet (24 m) high, with toothed leaves that turn yellow-orange to red in the fall. The peeling bark reveals mottled patches of neutral colors. While not fully immune, zelkova is resistant to Dutch elm disease and elm leaf beetles. Plant in full sun and in soil with even moisture and good drainage. Established trees tolerate drought. Zones 6–8. The cultivar 'Village Green' is grown for its symmetrical habit, fast growth, and cold-hardiness to Zone 5.

WHEN TO PRUNE: In late summer or fall.

HOW TO PRUNE: Needs little pruning. Remove dead wood and any crossing or rubbing limbs; also thin occasionally to reduce wind resistance. On trees along streets, sidewalks, or anywhere else where people might pass beneath, remove lower limbs gradually over several years.

PRUNING VINES

A pergola dripping with fragrant wisteria blossoms, a weathered fence laced with the blazing reds of Virginia creeper, a porch screened and shaded by Dutchman's pipe: These beautiful garden features represent some of the best of what vines have to offer. Many of the finest ideas for using vines in your landscape come from nature; others come from centuries of garden tradition. Either way, you can't go wrong. As you gain experience in growing vines, you'll find that they are some of the most forgiving plants in your landscape. They happily recover from winter damage and pruning mistakes. Don't worry if you need to cut them back to paint or replace a support; they'll spring back better than ever.

Whether you're choosing a new vine for that choice spot or contemplating a vine that you already have growing, it's important to know the vine's habits. For instance, vines may be annual, perennial, or woody; they may climb with tendrils, twining stems, aerial roots, or adhesive disks; they may flower on new stems or old wood from previous seasons. These different habits will have a great effect on how you support and train each plant. Your task with the pruning shears will also be different for each.

In this chapter, you'll learn how to choose the right kind of supporting structure to show your vines off to best advantage. You'll also find the techniques you'll need to prune and train all kinds of young and mature vines, as well as tips on rejuvenating old, overgrown vines for fresh new growth. The "Guide to Vines," starting on page 92, offers specific details on growing, pruning, and training 14 popular landscape vines.

Well-pruned vines add a special dimension of interest to any landscape. Some bear colorful flowers; others, including Virginia creeper (*Parthenocissus quinquefolia*), have beautiful foliage and outstanding fall color.

Vine Training Basics

Maybe you simply *must* have a honeysuckle for your yard but don't have anything for it to climb on. Or perhaps you have a plain fence that's crying out for a vine but don't know which vine to choose. Either way, matching a vine with the proper support is a critical part of successful vine training.

When matching a support and a vine, you'll want to keep these factors in mind:
• How does the vine climb?
• How vigorous is the vine?
• How strong is the support?
• What kind of maintenance will the support need?
The answers to these questions will help you make the best possible combination of vine and support.

How Vines Climb

Vines have developed several different strategies for clambering up a supporting structure.

Twining Vines Vines that climb by twining their stems around a support include wisteria and honeysuckle. Twining vines can climb a post, trellis, fence, or arbor, but they cannot scale a wall without something to wrap around. To grow a twining vine on a wall, provide it with wire supports or a mounted trellis.

Tendrils Vines that climb using modified leaves, called tendrils, include porcelain ampelopsis

Clematis wrap their leaf stalks around wires, netting, chain-link fences, or other support structures as they climb.

(*Ampelopsis brevipedunculata*), passionflowers (*Passiflora* spp.), and grapes. Clematis are similar in that they wrap their leaf stalks around a support much as tendrils do. These kinds of vines can usually climb the same kinds of structures as twining vines, although some appreciate more slender supports. Delicate tendrils have an easier time curling around chain-link fences, trellises with narrow laths, and netting- or wire-covered posts. If the tendrils can't wrap around a wider support, they may twine around each other and the plant stems, producing a tangled, floppy mess.

Clinging Vines Clinging vines hug walls and other vertical surfaces, clothing buildings and solid fences with their foliage. English ivy (*Hedera helix*), wintercreeper (*Euonymus fortunei*), and climbing hydrangea (*Hydrangea anomala* subsp. *petiolaris*) produce adhesive aerial rootlets along their stems. Trumpet vines (*Campsis* spp.), Virginia creeper (*Parthenocissus quinquefolia*), and Boston ivy (*P. cuspidata*) form adhesive disks at the ends of tendrils. When choosing a structure, remember that these vines need roughened vertical surfaces; they usually don't climb smooth structures like plastic trellises.

Vine Vigor and Support Strength

Part of selecting the right support is balancing the weight of the vine with the solidity of the structure. Thin plastic, wire, or wood trellises are fine for delicate vines like clematis, but they won't support more vigorous climbers. Sturdy posts, fences, and lattice structures provide ample support for most vines. Choose the stoutest of arbors, pergolas, or trellises for strong climbers like wisteria and trumpet vine, as these will become cumbersome and heavy with age.

Virginia creeper climbs with tendrils that are tipped with adhesive disks. It can clamber up many types of supports.

Can Vines and Walls Coexist?

Think very carefully before deciding to train clinging vines to the walls of your house. While the vines aren't inherently destructive, the aerial roots or adhesive disks can infiltrate already-soft mortar. If you remove a clinging vine that's been growing for many years, the exposed disintegrating mortar will be subject to further damage from wind and rain. At the very least, you'll be left with a mess of tiny rootlets stuck tight to the wall. These tenacious vines can also damage aluminum siding, leaving a spotting pattern when you pull them off the metal.

Aggressive climbers like wisteria are notorious for taking over anything in their path, pushing up asphalt shingles and roof tiles, and pulling down gutters and downspouts. Proper pruning can help to keep these ramblers in line, but it's laborious and time-consuming work.

The consensus is that vines and walls can and do coexist. But it's important to choose the vine carefully and, in some cases, to consider a support system that holds the vine away from the wall. Also be vigilant in training vines away from roofs, gutters, and downspouts to prevent damage.

Caring for mature vines can be a maintenance hassle. Be sure to consider how big the vine will get before you plant.

Support Maintenance

Carefully consider what kind of maintenance the support will need. Plastic and wire structures can be maintenance-free for years; wooden supports may need regular painting or staining. If you'll need to treat a wall or fence every few years, consider mounting a trellis 2 to 3 inches (5 to 7.5 cm) in front of it and growing the vine on that. The extra space will allow good air circulation behind the vine, which is better for the wall and healthier for your plant. Attach the base of the trellis to hinges, so you can unhook the panel and lower it away from the wall for easy painting.

Attaching Vines to Supports

Tendril climbers and clinging vines are generally trouble-free when it comes to training—once they get established, they find a support and stick to it. Twining vines, though, and a few less vigorous clingers will need a little help to get started on their climb.

One method of attachment is a figure-eight knot. Tie a length of soft twine (or other material that won't cut into a succulent stem) around the support, then tie the loose ends around the growing vine.

To attach a twining vine to a stone or brick wall, consider lead-headed vine clamps or similar lead hardware made especially for stone or brick. Depending on how hard the wall is, you may need to drill holes and cement in the hardware. If you're hesitant to disturb a stone or brick wall, consider the advantages of clinging vines, as they need no such attachment!

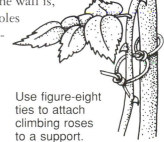

Use figure-eight ties to attach climbing roses to a support.

Honeysuckle is a true twining vine. It will eagerly wrap its stems around posts, fences, arbors, and even other plants!

On a wooden wall, you could attach the vine directly to rust-resistant galvanized screws or screw eyes with a figure-eight knot. Or— better yet—string wires vertically or horizontally between screws and train the vines to that. Remember that good air circulation is important for both the vine and the wall; try to leave at least 2 to 3 inches (5 to 7.5 cm) between the wires and the wall.

Training Climbers through Other Plants

Gardeners are always cautioned to give plants their space and not impose competition, so the option of training climbers onto other plants may seem suspect. In fact, anyone who has seen kudzu and other invasive vines choking out an entire landscape may view the prospect with trepidation. A highly competitive climber will surely weaken any shrubby partner, so give careful consideration to any such marriage.

With careful planning, though, growing vines through shrubs and small trees can produce great results. If you choose a shrub and vine that bloom at different times, you can effectively extend the season of interest in your landscape. By pairing a shrub and vine that bloom at the same time, you can add excitement, intrigue, or mayhem by having a shrub blooming with two different kinds—or colors—of flowers!

For best results, consider using a vine that you can cut down to the ground every year—perhaps a passion-

Create exciting combinations by allowing vines to scramble through shrubs. This pairing of mahonia (*Mahonia* sp.) and clematis offers year-round appeal.

flower, porcelain ampelopsis, or a clematis, which blooms on the current season's growth. Annual vines are also an option, though you should choose one that doesn't seed itself aggressively (as morning glories will!).

Shrubs and small trees that lend themselves well to this treatment include viburnums (*Viburnum* spp.), lilacs (*Syringa* spp.), sweet mock orange (*Philadelphus coronarius*), beautybush (*Kolkwitzia amabilis*), wintersweet (*Chimonanthus praecox*), and cornelian cherry (*Cornus mas*). For a classic combination, try fountain buddleia (*Buddleia alternifolia*) with a later-blooming clematis, like *Clematis viticella* or scarlet clematis (*C. texensis*).

When using a shrub as a support, it's best to let the shrub get established for a few years before adding the competition of a vine. Then plant the vine in a well-prepared hole about 18 inches (45 cm) out from the base of the shrub. Use a string or twigs to lead the climber up into the shrub.

Attaching a Trellis to a Wall

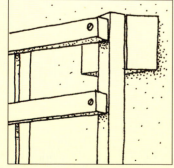

Use a block of wood to hold the trellis away from the wall.

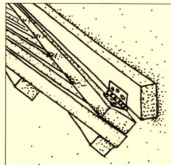

Hinge the bottom of the trellis for easy wall maintenance.

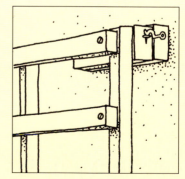

Secure the top of a hinged trellis to the wall with a hook and eye.

Clinging vines generally don't need much maintenance—just light annual trimming to keep them in good shape.

Pruning and Training Vines

The reasons to prune vines are as various as the vines themselves. You may want to limit the growth of a vigorous vine or restart an overgrown one by rejuvenating it. You may wish to improve a vine's flowering or fruiting or to trim it away from windows, doors, or downspouts. The climbing and flowering habits of your particular vine determine the best pruning strategy.

Climbing Habit Considerations

The way your vine grows has a great effect on how and how often you'll need to prune.

Twining Vines Twining vines generate most of their new growth from their tips, often becoming bare at the base. On some twiners—like hops (*Humulus lupulus*)—you may cut the vines back to the ground every year. On heavier vines, such as wisteria, you'll cut back the new growth to three or four buds. Train the new growth as needed to reclimb the supports. If a stem of a twining vine comes loose from its support, you can simply reattach it, and it will resume its climb.

Clinging Vines Clinging vines usually only need annual thinning or cleanup pruning to keep them in good shape. If part of a clinging vine comes off of a wall or other support, cut off or tie in the loose stems; their disks or aerial roots won't reattach. Clinging vines tend to be relatively permanent landscape features; they seldom, if ever, need to be cut back to the ground with rejuvenation pruning.

Tendril-climbing Vines These climbers fall into a gray area between twining and clinging vines. Some, like grapes, need to be trimmed just lightly; others, such as passionflowers (*Passiflora* spp.), may need to be cut back hard every year. The approach you take generally depends on the flowering and fruiting habits of that particular vine. The individual entries in the "Guide to Vines," starting on page 92, will tell you the best way to prune.

Roses The so-called climbing roses don't use any of these previous techniques to scramble up supports. Instead, they use their thorns to catch onto a structure and hold themselves up. In the garden, you'll need to tie the canes to whatever support you use. For complete pruning and training details, see "Pruning Climbing Roses" on page 139.

Flowering Habit Factors

As with flowering shrubs and trees, flowering time often determines the season for pruning vines. Prune vines that bloom on the current season's wood during the dormant season. Examples include porcelain ampelopsis (*Ampelopsis brevipedunculata*) and passionflowers. Also use the dormant season to rejuvenate any vine or to do major cleanup pruning.

Prune vines that bloom on the previous season's wood after they finish blooming. Examples include wisteria, honeysuckle, and star jasmine (*Trachelospermum jasminoides*). Try to complete this pruning within a month after plants finish flowering to allow them to form next year's flower buds.

Clematis are a tricky group to give general guidelines for, since some species and hybrids bloom on new

Vigorous annual pruning will help passionflowers bloom heavily. Cut the stems close to ground level in late winter.

wood and some bloom on last season's wood. For specific guidelines, see the Clematis entry on page 95.

Early Training

The key to successful early vine training is having the support system in place at planting time. Vines have a way of growing by leaps and bounds while you're waiting for a good time to set that post or put up the trellis. Moreover, many vines—such as clematis—can be brittle and will break if you handle them carelessly. Unsupported twining vines will wrap around themselves, leaving you with a tangled mess or a patience-trying disentangling job.

If the vine you are planting is bareroot, cut all top growth to the ground after planting. This will give the roots a chance to get established before top growth starts to grow.

After planting a container-grown vine, first remove any dead stems that you see. If you'll be training your vine to an overhead arch or pergola, thin away all but the stem or stems you'll be training up the post. Otherwise, select three

Wisterias need a sturdy support and routine pruning several times a year to look their best and to flower generously.

to five of the strongest shoots and remove the others. Cut the selected shoots back by one-half. Many new shoots will appear following this initial pruning. Pinch the tips if you want your vine to be fully branched from the base. Train the new shoots to climb the support you've provided.

On any kind of vine, pinch out the tips where you want growth to fill in or where you need the vine to branch. Use thinning cuts to manage growth that becomes too heavy or thick. Never hesitate to snip away dead or tattered growth or clinging vine growth that comes away from a wall. Regular pinching, snipping, and training when plants are young will make pruning the mature vine much less of a chore.

Pruning an Overgrown Vine

Every now and then you'll be faced with a long-neglected vine that's a hopeless tangle of big, woody stems. While you might be able to pick your way through the mess and remove the dead growth, the remaining stems often end up much worse for the wear.

Fear not. One of the finer qualities of vines is their ability to respond to rejuvenation pruning—the kind where you cut the entire overgrown mess to the ground and start again. Remember that the root system has been growing for years and—especially during the dormant season—stores much in the way of energy reserves. Take advantage of this stored energy by cutting the vine down in late winter. Leave a few of the newer stalks—if there are any—at the base of the vine. When growth begins in the spring and the vine sends up vigorous new shoots, remove all but the few that you'll need to train up the supports. Train them as you would any new vine.

If you grow two climbers together, choose ones that have similar pruning needs to make maintenance easier.

Clinging vines use adhesive rootlets to attach to walls.

Some climbers use structures called tendrils to grab supports.

Twining vines wrap themselves—stems and all—around a support.

Pruning Established Vines

After a vine has filled out and covered the space you want, most of your pruning will consist of snipping back any growth that grows out of bounds. Remove dead, diseased, winter-damaged, or tattered growth regularly. On clinging vines, never hesitate to remove growth that has come loose, as it is unlikely it will reattach itself. Use heading cuts to encourage branching on growth that seems open and leggy; use thinning cuts on growth that seems heavy and crowded. Tidy up unruly growth as needed.

You may choose to cut some established vines to the ground each year. Good candidates are those that grow vigorously and bloom on new growth, such as passionflowers and some of the clematis. Vines managed in this manner can be counted on to bloom profusely, and they require less investment in training time. Let them grow each year into a delightful jumble! Your one annual pruning will keep them in bounds.

Big woody vines such as wisteria and trumpet vine (*Campsis radicans*) often need pruning several times a year. Prune these vigorous vines both after flowering and during the dormant season to keep the flowers coming and the vine from taking over the neighborhood.

For specifics on how and when to prune any established vine, see the individual plant entries in the "Guide to Vines," starting on page 92.

You can trim out dead, damaged, or wayward growth anytime to keep a vine healthy and well shaped.

Vigorous vines, including trumpet creeper, require trimming several times a year to keep them in bounds.

Actinidia spp.   Actinidiaceae

KIWI

Kiwi vines climb by twining their vines around a support. They can tolerate hard pruning, so prune and trim as needed to keep them in their allotted space.

DESCRIPTION: Kiwis are deciduous twining vines that have attractive foliage and edible fruit. To get the fruit, you usually need to grow both male and female plants; a few cultivars, such as *A. arguta* 'Issai', are self-fruitful. Kiwis grow best in full sun or partial shade.

A. arguta (hardy kiwi): Rampant grower; height 23–30 feet (6.9–9 m). White or greenish white flowers bloom in May and June, but are hidden by the foliage; grape-sized fruits develop later in the season. Zones 3–8.

A. kolomikta (hardy kiwi): Climbs to 15–20 feet (4.5–6 m). White to pink markings can appear on leaves of mature plants; shade, heat, and very fertile soil can inhibit this stunning coloration. Zones 4–8.

WHEN TO PRUNE: Late summer to early spring is the best time for heavy pruning. You may also thin the vines midway through the growing season.

HOW TO PRUNE: Cut fall- or spring-planted vines back to four or five buds. Guide the new shoots to the support as needed. If you're growing the vines for their leaves, simply trim and thin as needed to keep them in bounds. For best fruit production follow the pruning tips in the Kiwi entry on page 127.

SPECIAL TIPS: Provide support in the form of a sturdy trellis, arbor, or fence. Be sure the support has some vertical posts or wires for the vine to twine on as it climbs.

Akebia quinata   Lardizabalaceae

FIVE-LEAVED AKEBIA

Five-leaved akebia wraps its fast-growing, twining vines around almost any vertical support. Thin out dead, damaged, or unwanted growth as needed after flowering.

DESCRIPTION: Five-leaved akebia is a vigorous grower useful for fast cover on trellises, arbors, pergolas, or fences. It can climb to 20–40 feet (6–12 m) by twining on its supports. The dark, blue-green, compound leaves have five leaflets and give the vine a fine texture. The inconspicuous purple flowers bloom as the leaves develop in spring. Widely tolerant of different sites, five-leaved akebia grows well in dry or moist conditions, sun or shade. It is deciduous in Northern climates and evergreen in the southern end of its range; Zones 4–8.

WHEN TO PRUNE: Choose late winter or early spring (before growth begins) for renewal pruning. Wait until summer (after flowering) for thinning or cleanup.

HOW TO PRUNE: For general maintenance and cleanup, use thinning cuts to remove dead or tattered growth. Control rampant or overgrown vines by cutting the whole thing back to the ground.

SPECIAL TIPS: Provide a support with vertical wires or posts so the vine can twine and climb.

Ampelopsis brevipedunculata   Vitaceae

PORCELAIN VINE

Porcelain vine quickly scrambles upward by coiling its tendrils around any thin support. Prune the previous season's shoots back in late winter or early spring to encourage new growth.

DESCRIPTION: Porcelain vine is a fast-growing deciduous vine that climbs by tendrils to a height of 15 feet (4.5 m). The species has dark green, three-lobed leaves; the cultivar 'Maximowiczii' bears finely dissected leaves. Inconspicuous flowers bloom midsummer on new growth, followed by porcelain-like, $^3/_8$-inch (9 mm) fruits in yellow to pale lilac to dark blue. Plant in full sun and well-drained soil. Limiting the root zone—by planting in a pot or perhaps in shallow, rocky soil—can help to optimize fruiting. Zones 4–8.

WHEN TO PRUNE: In late winter or early spring before growth begins.

HOW TO PRUNE: Porcelain vine blooms and sets fruit on the current season's growth. Hard pruning—cutting the previous season's growth back to two or three buds—will encourage strong new growth and good fruiting. To rejuvenate an overgrown vine, cut all the stems to the ground.

SPECIAL TIPS: Provide support in the form of a trellis, arbor, or fence.

Aristolochia durior Aristolochiaceae

DUTCHMAN'S-PIPE

The twining stems of Dutchman's-pipe readily climb trellises, posts, arbors, and other vertical supports. After flowering, thin out any damaged or unwanted growth.

DESCRIPTION: This twining vine has large heart- or kidney-shaped, dark green leaves that can be as much as 10 inches (25 cm) long. In moist, well-drained soil and full sun or partial shade, Dutchman's-pipe can grow to 20–30 feet (6–9 m). Large smoking-pipe-shaped flowers bloom in the leaf axils in late spring or early summer. Young flowers are yellow-green; they quickly turn brownish purple as they age. Zones 4–8.

WHEN TO PRUNE: Prune after flowering to clean up the vine and keep it in bounds. Prune in winter to rejuvenate an old vine.

HOW TO PRUNE: Use thinning cuts to remove unwanted or tattered growth. Rejuvenate by cutting the entire vine to the ground.

SPECIAL TIPS: Grow Dutchman's-pipe on an arbor, trellis, or pergola. Provide vertical posts or wires to give the vine something to twine around as it climbs.

Campsis spp. Bignoniaceae

TRUMPET VINES

Trumpet vine uses root-like holdfasts to cling to walls, arbors, pergolas—just about any sturdy structure that's available! Cut the shoots back hard in late winter or early spring.

DESCRIPTION: These deciduous vines cling to surfaces with root-like holdfasts. They can climb rapidly to 40 feet (12 m) or more with heavy, woody stems. The leaves are pinnately compound. Showy, trumpet-like flowers bloom throughout the summer and into fall. Trumpet vines prefer full sun and can adapt to a wide range of soil conditions. *C. radicans* (trumpet vine, trumpet creeper): Clusters of red to orange, 2-inch (5 cm) long flowers. Zones 4–9.

C. x *tagliabuana* 'Madame Galen' ('Madam Galen' trumpet vine): Similar but with larger flowers. Zones 6–9.

WHEN TO PRUNE: In late winter or early spring, before growth begins.

HOW TO PRUNE: This vigorous grower can clamber over just about everything in its path! To control the growth and promote flowering, prune every year; cut the previous year's shoots back to two or three buds.

SPECIAL TIPS: Because it climbs with holdfasts, trumpet vine can grow on walls as well as on arbors or pergolas. Whatever support you provide, be sure that it can bear significant weight.

CLEMATIS

Clematis vines climb by wrapping their leaf stalks around a support. Thin wooden stakes, wire or mesh trellises, and chain-link fences provide the right conditions for easy climbing.

The hybrid clematis 'Niobe' blooms in early summer and again in early fall. To encourage vigorous growth, trim shoot tips back to the first pair of plump buds in late winter.

DESCRIPTION: Clematis are a diverse group of deciduous or evergreen vines. They can climb 5–18 feet (1.5–5.4 m) high by wrapping their leaf stalks around thin supports. The leaves are heart- or lance-shaped. The species clematis normally have small flowers in the shape of stars, saucers, or bells; the hybrids usually bear large, flat blooms 3–6 inches (7.5–15 cm) wide. Feathery seed heads follow the flowers.

Plant clematis at the base of the support on which they will grow. (The vines tend to be brittle and break when handled, so resist the temptation to wait and install your support later.) Clematis need full sun for their leaves but shade for their roots. Site your vine near a shrub or other object that will provide low shade, and mulch well.

WHEN TO PRUNE: The timing will depend on whether your clematis bloom on the previous year's stems or the current year's shoots (new growth). Prune those that bloom on the previous year's wood just after flowering. Prune those that bloom on new growth in late winter or early spring before growth begins.

HOW TO PRUNE: Clematis pruning may seem complicated, but it doesn't have to be. The trick is to know where your particular vine blooms. To find out, check the plant tag or its catalog description, or just watch your plant for a year and see how it acts.

EARLY-BLOOMING CLEMATIS: Vines that bloom only in late spring or early summer produce their flowers on leafless stalks that come directly from the previous season's stems. Prune the current season's shoots back to two or three pairs of buds after flowering. Reclaim an overgrown vine of this type by cutting it back hard after bloom.

REBLOOMING CLEMATIS: Clematis that bloom in early summer and again later in the year need a different approach. Prune the shoot tips back to the first pair of plump buds in late winter to early spring (before the buds start to grow). To reclaim an overgrown vine, cut all of the stems down to the lowest pair of strong buds in late winter or early spring; you'll lose the early bloom but get a bigger crop of flowers later in the season.

SUMMER- AND FALL-BLOOMING CLEMATIS: Some clematis bloom only on the current season's stems, generally in summer or fall. Prune these types down to the lowest pair of strong buds on each stem in late winter or early spring.

Gelsemium sempervirens   Loganiaceae

CAROLINA JESSAMINE

Evergreen Carolina jessamine wraps its thin, twining stems around posts, trellises, wires, and other vertical supports. Trim as needed after flowering to encourage branching.

DESCRIPTION: Carolina jessamine is an evergreen, wiry, twining vine that may grow 10–20 feet (3–6 m) tall. The shiny, dark green leaves often take on a purplish cast in winter. Yellow, fragrant, funnel-shaped flowers begin blooming between February and April (depending on your climate) and continue blooming sporadically through the summer and fall. All parts are poisonous when ingested. Although Carolina jessamine will tolerate some shade, it grows and blooms best in full sun and moist, well-drained soil. Zones 7–9.

WHEN TO PRUNE: After flowering.

HOW TO PRUNE: Cut the vine back hard to keep it full. To rejuvenate an old or spindly looking vine, prune it back to the ground.

SPECIAL TIPS: Posts and trellises make good supports. Provide vertical wires to guide the vines to twine upward.

Hedera helix   Araliaceae

ENGLISH IVY

English ivy clings to walls and trees with sturdy aerial rootlets. Trim as needed to control the shape and spread of the vines and to promote denser growth.

DESCRIPTION: This vigorous, evergreen vine climbs and clings using holdfasts on aerial rootlets. Grow it as either a climbing vine (to 90 feet [27 m] high) or a groundcover (about 6 inches [15 cm] high). English ivy has shiny three- or five-lobed leaves, often with decorative veination or variegation. On mature growth, the vine becomes quite woody and heavy, leaves become entire—lacking those three or five lobes—and inconspicuous black berries persist through the fall and winter.

Grow ivy in partial to dense shade and in well-drained soil. In a severe winter, the foliage may burn and brown, especially if the vine is exposed to sun. The cultivar 'Baltica' is known and grown for its hardiness; 'Thorndale' is grown for its handsome white veination. Zones 5–9. Smaller-leaved cultivars, such as 'Needlepoint' and 'Gold Heart' are often less cold-hardy (usually Zones 6–9) but can be useful in the landscape for their fine texture.

WHEN TO PRUNE: To promote denser growth, prune in late winter or early spring before growth begins; otherwise, prune anytime.

HOW TO PRUNE: Use heading cuts to promote thicker, denser growth. Use thinning cuts to shape or train. If you find the mature growth on an old vine to be undesirable, prune it out.

SPECIAL TIPS: Grow on walls or other rough-surfaced vertical supports, as well as on tree trunks.

Hydrangea anomala subsp. *petiolaris* Hydrangeaceae

CLIMBING HYDRANGEA

Climbing hydrangea clings to tree trunks, stone walls, and other rough surfaces with root-like holdfasts. Prune in early spring to thin out loose or damaged stems.

DESCRIPTION: This clinging deciduous vine climbs with root-like holdfasts to heights of 60 feet (18 m) or more. White, fragrant, hydrangea-like flowers bloom in early summer. The woody stems have peeling bark, revealing a cinnamon brown inner bark. The handsome, dark green foliage drops in fall without changing color. Plant in sun or shade and in rich, moist, well-drained soil. Zones 4–7.

WHEN TO PRUNE: In early spring.

HOW TO PRUNE: Use thinning cuts to remove loose, hanging stems or tattered foliage or to train. Use heading cuts to thicken growth.

SPECIAL TIPS: Grow climbing hydrangea on rough vertical surfaces.

Lonicera spp. Caprifoliaceae

HONEYSUCKLES

Honeysuckles climb by twining their stems around vertical supports. Trim after flowering to encourage branching on spindly vines, or prune heavily to control rampant growth.

DESCRIPTION: Honeysuckles are deciduous, evergreen, or semi-evergreen twining vines popular for their showy—and sometimes fragrant—flowers. Plant in full sun to partial shade and in well-drained soil. *L.* x *heckrottii* (goldflame honeysuckle, everblooming honeysuckle): Height up to 20 feet (6 m). Bears large clusters of pinkish purple-and-yellow flowers from early summer until early fall. Zones 4–9. *L. japonica* (Japanese honeysuckle): Rampant grower; height to 60 feet (18 m). The shiny green leaves are evergreen in the South and semi-evergreen in the North, often bronzing in winter. Fragrant, white, trumpet-like flowers bloom sporadically through the growing season and turn yellow as they age. Has become a troublesome weed in many parts of the United States. Zones 4–9. *L. sempervirens* (trumpet honeysuckle): Height to 20 feet (6 m). Its pairs of leaves are fused with each other at the base; they retain their waxy, bluish green color throughout the year in the South. Scarlet or yellow-orange flower clusters bloom in summer. Zones 4–9.

WHEN TO PRUNE: After flowering.

HOW TO PRUNE: Use heading cuts to encourage young plants to fill in. Prune heavily to reduce the vigor of a rampant plant.

SPECIAL TIPS: Provide the support of a fence, wall, or arbor with vertical posts or wires.

Parthenocissus spp.   Vitaceae

WOODBINES

Woodbines can scale walls and fences by clinging with adhesive disks on the ends of tendrils. To direct the growth, trim them anytime except late winter or early spring.

DESCRIPTION: These deciduous vines climb with adhesive disks on tendrils to heights of 30–50 feet (9–15 m). They are known for their great fall color in shades of red and burgundy and for their blue-black, grape-like fruits that are revealed after the leaves have fallen. Give them full sun or shade and practically any soil that isn't waterlogged.

P. quinquefolia (Virginia creeper): Has palmately compound leaves with five leaflets. Zones 3–9.

P. tricuspidata (Boston ivy): Has simple, three-lobed leaves. Zones 4–8.

WHEN TO PRUNE: Anytime except late winter or early spring, when rising sap is likely to bleed. While this bleeding isn't harmful, most gardeners consider it to be undesirable.

HOW TO PRUNE: Use heading cuts to encourage young vines to fill in. Trim established vines as needed to control growth or to train.

SPECIAL TIPS: Because of their method of climbing, woodbines are good for covering stone, brick, or wooden walls and fences.

Passiflora spp.   Passifloraceae

PASSIONFLOWERS

Passionflowers scramble upward by wrapping their tendrils around thin supports, such as railings, guide wires, and trellises. Cut vines back almost to the ground in late winter.

DESCRIPTION: Passionflowers are semi-evergreen or evergreen vines that climb by twining tendrils to 20 feet (6 m) high. The leaves are three- or five-lobed, and the unique flowers are colorful and individually dramatic. Plant in well-drained but moist soil and light shade.

P. caerulea (blue passionflower): May have blue, pale pink, or white summer flowers that are mildly fragrant. The five-lobed leaves are evergreen in the southern parts of the plant's usual hardiness range (Zones 8–10).

P. incarnata (wild passionflower, maypop): Blooms in midsummer to early fall and produces sweet, edible yellow fruits. The flowers on this southeastern native are mostly purplish. Generally hardy in Zones 6–10.

WHEN TO PRUNE: In late winter.

HOW TO PRUNE: Because passionflowers bloom on the current season's growth, they flower best when growing vigorously. Cut the previous year's shoots close to ground level. Pull out unwanted sucker shoots.

SPECIAL TIPS: Support passionflowers with a fence, trellis, or post; add vertical wires to guide the vines upward.

| *Trachelospermum jasminoides* Apocynaceae | *Wisteria* spp. Leguminosae |

STAR JASMINE

WISTERIA

Evergreen star jasmine scales vertical supports with twining stems. Prune after flowering to promote new flowering stems for next year and to keep the vine in bounds.

Wisteria is a fast-growing twining vine that needs a sturdy support and heavy pruning. Cut the previous season's shoots back in late winter or early spring; trim again after flowering.

DESCRIPTION: Star jasmine, also known as confederate jasmine, is a twining evergreen vine that can climb to 12 feet (3.6 m). It also makes an attractive groundcover. It begins blooming in May or June, then continues sporadically through the growing season, bearing fragrant, white, five-petaled flowers. The foliage is dark green and waxy. Provide partial or full shade and well-drained soil. Zones 8–9.

WHEN TO PRUNE: After flowering.

HOW TO PRUNE: As with other landscape plants that bloom on the current season's stems, vigorous growth is the key to keeping the blooms coming. Clip climbing vines as needed to train them or to keep them from outgrowing their space. Rejuvenate an old, overgrown vine by cutting it to the ground. Shear groundcover plantings every few years to keep them vigorous and neat.

SPECIAL TIPS: To grow star jasmine as a vine, support it with a trellis or fence; add vertical wires to guide the stems upward.

DESCRIPTION: These deciduous, twining vines can easily grow to 30 feet (9 m) or much more if given the opportunity. They are known and loved for their pendant, violet-blue flower clusters that begin to bloom in late spring. They prefer full sun and well-drained, fertile soil.

W. floribunda (Japanese wisteria): Has large flower clusters. Choose the cultivar 'Alba' for its white flowers; 'Rosea' has rose pink flowers. Zones 5–9.

W. sinensis (Chinese wisteria): Has somewhat smaller flower clusters and is slightly less cold-hardy than Japanese wisteria. Zones 6–9.

WHEN TO PRUNE: In late winter or early spring before growth begins and after flowering.

HOW TO PRUNE: During the dormant season, cut shoots from the previous year back to about three buds. After bloom, remove spent flowers and do any cleanup pruning that is necessary to shape the plant and keep it in bounds. Remove sucker shoots as they appear through the growing season.

SPECIAL TIPS: When training wisterias, keep in mind that Chinese wisteria twines counterclockwise around a support and Japanese wisteria twines clockwise. As they can become quite massive and heavy with time, be sure that your support—trellis, arbor, or pergola—is very strong. Don't let wisteria climb up drainpipes; the vines can easily pull down pipes and gutters.

PRUNING FRUITS, NUTS, AND BERRIES

Sound pruning and training practices help to keep your fruit trees and bushes healthy, attractive, and productive. Exactly when, how, and how much you'll have to prune depends on many different factors, including when the plants flower, where the fruit forms, and how susceptible the plants are to disease. It sounds complicated, but it really isn't. This chapter will give you the details you need to prune many different kinds of fruits confidently and effectively.

Training fruits and berries involves a variety of techniques, including staking, branch spreading, and some pruning. During the first 3 to 5 years of a plant's life, good training is a vital part of shaping it into a strong, high-yielding mature tree, shrub, or vine. Some bush fruits, like blueberries, need minimal training; they bear well in their natural form. Fruit trees and grapes, on the other hand, require regular and careful training to produce the best possible yields.

Once a tree begins to bear steadily, pruning becomes more important to keep plants healthy and vigorous. The various pruning practices described in this chapter will help you to promote strong fruit-bearing branches and the formation of good-quality fruit.

If you are faced with an overmature or neglected fruit tree, don't despair! The tips and techniques here will help you to determine if the tree's basic structure is sound and if it's worth the time and energy you'll need to work it back into good shape. You'll also learn what *not* to do when trying to coax an old fruit tree back into a productive life.

In the pages that follow, you'll find the basic techniques you need to train and prune just about any fruit tree or fruiting vine. Pages on specific fruit crops offer details on the methods that work best for particular plants. When you are ready to prune, flip to the quick-reference "Guide to Fruiting Plants," starting on page 120, for the basic facts on training and pruning 23 different fruit and nut crops.

Careful, well-timed pruning will help your plants develop vigorous, productive fruiting growth. While most fruit crops need more pruning than other landscape plants, the taste of homegrown fruit is worth the effort.

Fruit Training and Pruning Basics

The words training and pruning are sometimes used interchangeably, but—especially with regard to fruit trees—they're not the same. Training does involve some pruning, but it also includes a variety of other techniques, such as staking and branch spreading. Good training on young trees creates a strong framework of limbs that can support abundant future crops. As trees get older and begin to bear fruit, regular pruning helps to keep plants vigorous, healthy, and productive.

The same basic training and pruning techniques apply to many kinds of fruit trees, including apples, pears, peaches, and cherries. Bush fruits, like blueberries and currants, and grapevines have their own particular training practices; they are covered later in this chapter.

Cherries are among the easiest fruit crops to grow since they don't require much pruning or thinning.

Training Young Fruit Trees

Good training starts the day you plant your young fruit tree and continues through the next few years. For training a freestanding fruit tree, follow the steps below. Espalier-trained fruit trees—those grown flat against a fence or wall—need slightly different care; see "Shaping Espalier" on page 150 for details.

At Planting Time If you bought your young tree bareroot from a mail-order nursery, it may have already been pruned; be sure to read the packing materials to find out. If you're planting a bareroot or container-grown tree that hasn't yet been pruned, cut the main stem back to a bud about 24 to 30 inches (60 to 75 cm) above the ground. This may seem like a drastic step, but it will encourage the production of needed side branches. If the tree already has some side branches, also cut them back by about one-third to outward-facing buds.

First Summer after Planting When the branches are 12 to 18 inches (30 to 45 cm) long, it's time to start training the framework of your tree. Look carefully at the branching structure, then follow the pruning recommendations here. Don't worry if you end up cutting off many or even all of the branches; it's not worth keeping poorly placed branches if you want a strong, healthy mature tree. If you have only one or two branches left, prune them back to the main stem and start again with the instructions under "At Planting Time" above.

The central leader or modified central leader system is commonly used for training young apple trees.

It may seem drastic, but heavy pruning on young fruit trees will encourage stronger growth.

Some plants produce their fruits on compact growths called spurs; others form fruits near the stem tips.

- Remove all dead or damaged wood as it appears.
- If two or more branches have sprouted from the same spot, prune out the weaker one.
- If two limbs are growing opposite each other, keep the best-placed one and prune out the other.
- If one branch is directly over another branch, keep the best-placed one and remove the other one.
- Where two branches are crossing or rubbing, prune out either one.

Of the remaining branches, choose three or four well-spaced ones for the permanent framework. These branches should all point in different directions and be separated up and down the trunk by 4 to 8 inches (10 to 20 cm) of stem. Prune out any unwanted side branches, but don't cut out the central shoot yet.

Before you finish this pruning session, decide which training style—central leader or open center—you're going to use. The form you choose will determine how much more pruning you need to do now and what kinds of cuts you'll make. The individual entries in the "Guide to Fruiting Plants," starting on page 120, will tell you which training style is best for your particular crop. You'll also find specific tips for training and pruning apples, peaches and nectarines, pears, cherries, plums, and nut trees in the pages that follow.

Training to a Central Leader

Regular central leader training produces an upright, symmetrical tree with a continuous center trunk. Modified central leader training is similar, but you'll eventually cut out the central shoot. Central leader or modified central leader training is generally the method of choice for guiding the growth of apples, European pears, sweet cherries, and European plums.

First Summer after Planting As you're selecting and establishing the main framework branches, leave the main shoot (the central leader) uncut. Spread the main side branches as explained in "Tree Training Tips" on page 105 to encourage strong branch angles.

First Winter after Planting Thin out any shoots that are growing at a narrow angle and competing with the central leader. Cut the main branches back by one-third to one-half to encourage side branches. If the central leader has grown very tall, you may want to cut it back to encourage side branching; this will create a modified central leader form. Prune it to a bud that's about 2 feet (60 cm) above the point where the uppermost branch joins the trunk. If the central leader looks in proportion with the rest of the tree, leave it uncut.

Second Summer after Planting When the central leader has produced new side branches that are 12 to 18 inches (30 to 45 cm) long, it's time to choose three or four more main branches. The lowest of these new branches should be roughly 18 inches (45 cm) above the highest branch in the first set. Choose new branches that are evenly spaced in a spiral around the trunk, so they won't crowd each other or shade the branches below. Spread these branches as needed. Cut off any unwanted branches at the main stem. Also remove or spread any watersprouts (shoots that grow up from the trunk or side branches) and remove all suckers (upright shoots that grow at the base of the trunk).

Second Winter after Planting In late winter or early spring, shorten the side branches by trimming back one-third to one-half of the previous season's growth. Also thin out any shoots that are growing at a narrow angle and competing with the central leader.

As your tree ages, you may have to remove older, damaged limbs. Making a proper cut will help the tree recover.

If the central leader has grown out of proportion with the rest of the tree, head it back as explained under "First Winter after Planting" on page 103.

Aftercare During the next two or three summers, select new tiers of branches as described in "Second Summer after Planting" on page 103. By the time the tree starts to bear fruit, you'll have established a sound framework of strong branches.

If you are growing a grafted tree, be especially careful to remove suckers that spring up at the base of the plant.

In following years, continue with mainly mid- to late-summer pruning. Use thinning cuts to remove downward-pointing branches and crowded stems to keep the tree open to light and air. Rub or cut off any suckers. On spur-bearing plants, trim back vigorous upward-growing shoots to ⅛- to ¼-inch (3 to 6 mm) stubs; these will form fruiting spurs. If you notice a "hole" in the overall shape of the tree, prune in late winter to head back branches around the empty space. Make your cuts just above buds that face toward the hole. Remove dead wood any time during the season.

Training to an Open Center

Training fruit trees to an open center or vase shape limits a tree's height, making it easily accessible for pruning, harvesting, and pest control. This system is commonly used on apricots, Asian pears, peaches, nectarines, tart cherries, and Japanese plums.

First Summer after Planting After you have selected the three or four main branches (as explained in "Training Young Fruit Trees" on page 102), cut off the center shoot just above the uppermost branch. Prune the main branches back by about one-third to encourage side branches.

Second Spring after Planting In midspring (when the leaves are beginning to emerge), trim back the previous season's shoots by about one-third to promote more side branching.

Aftercare Now that the basic framework is established, you won't have much training to do. At bloom time, trim all of the previous season's growth back by one-third. This will encourage the tree to keep producing new fruit-bearing growth. Remove any dead wood and watersprouts. Thin out crowded shoots to keep the center of the plant open to light and air.

Once plants start to bear, thin out one-third of the

Training to an Open Center

The summer after planting, remove the center shoot; trim side branches.

The second spring after planting, trim the previous season's shoots.

On bearing trees, thin one-third of the longest shoots at bloom time.

longest sideshoots at bloom time each year, cutting them back by about half of their total length. During the summer, remove dead wood, watersprouts, and crowded growth to allow for good air circulation.

Pruning an Overgrown or Neglected Tree

If you've inherited a neglected fruit tree, don't be tempted to grab a saw and just start cutting. First, try to figure out what basic structure (if any) the tree was trained to when it was younger. Central leader and modified central leader trees will have some kind of main trunk that extends upward through several tiers of branches. Open center trees usually have just a short main trunk that ends in three or four outward-spreading limbs. If you can identify a basic structure, it will give you some shape to work toward as you reclaim the tree. If you can't see any structure, you may have to create one as you go. The individual plant entries will tell you which training form is best for your particular plant.

Whether you're pruning back to an existing structure or creating a new one, don't try to do it all at once. Sudden, heavy pruning will bring on a crop of watersprouts like you've never seen before!

Start by removing dead or dying branches at any time of the year. Gradually—over a period of 3 to 4 years—prune in the dormant season to:

- Remove crossing or rubbing branches.
- Thin crowded stems to open the center to light and air; this will promote flowering and discourage diseases.
- Begin to remove any major branches that are shading others; take out only one or two each year.
- Head back long, weak limbs to strengthen them and encourage branching.

Each summer, remove about one-third of the watersprouts and suckers until they are all under control. Over time, this approach will gradually restore your tree to a new, productive existence.

Thinning crowded fruits will encourage even ripening and help ensure a good crop each year.

With a little careful pruning, dwarf and semidwarf apple trees can produce generous crops in a small space.

Training and Pruning Apple Trees

Even if they didn't produce a useful crop, apples would be worthwhile landscape plants for their beautiful display of sweet-smelling, pink-blushed white spring flowers. Happily, they can also provide generous fall crops of juicy fruits for fresh eating or cooking. With some careful pruning, you can help to ensure great yields and reduce the potential for disease problems as well. Good pruning will also promote balanced harvests, so you won't have a heavy crop one year and little or no fruit the next (a characteristic of some trees known as "alternate bearing").

Basic central leader training (as explained in "Training to a Central Leader" on page 103) works well for most apple trees. If you have full-sized (standard) apple trees, modified central leader or open

Late winter or early spring is the best time to do most of your apple tree pruning.

Apple Pruning Calendar

Here are some guidelines to help you decide what needs to be pruned and when to do it.

Late Winter or Early Spring Thin for form and head back branches that need stiffening. Remove dead or diseased wood. Thin tip-bearing types to renew bearing wood and to reduce the load on any weak branches. On spur types, head back sideshoots and trim shoot tips to promote the formation of more fruiting spurs. Thin old spurs and any crowded branches to get even distribution of sunlight to the center of the tree.

Late Spring and Summer Thin developing fruits to 6 to 8 inches (15 to 20 cm) apart after "June drop" (when some of the fruit falls off on its own). Clip or twist off the small fruits. Thin as needed to keep the center of the tree open to light and air. Remove suckers and watersprouts. Stop pruning by midsummer. If the tree bears a particularly heavy crop, some of the branches may start to bend downward. Prop up these sagging branches with a forked stick until after harvest.

center training may help to keep the size under control for easier care and harvesting.

If you really want to get the best possible yields, you can tailor your pruning to match your particular type of tree. Apple trees can be divided into two basic groups, depending on whether they bear their fruits on compact growths called spurs or on the tips of the branches. Read the descriptions below and see which one best matches the habits of your particular tree; then train and prune accordingly.

As you prune your apples, keep in mind that apple wood tends to be very fragrant when burned. Collect your prunings and allow them to dry for sweet-smelling fireplace or wood-stove kindling.

Spur-bearing Types

Spur-bearing apples are usually upright in form. If left unpruned, spur-bearers tend to form narrow branch angles and have sparse branches. The fruits form on long-lived spurs, which usually develop on the branches fairly close to the trunk. 'Starkrimson',

Remove some of the developing fruits to allow the remaining apples room to expand and ripen without crowding.

Most apples don't need much pruning during the summer; just thin the fruit and remove suckers and watersprouts.

'Jonagold', and 'Red Delicious' are just a few of the apples that fall into this category.

Train spur-bearers to a central leader, spreading branches that have narrow angles (see "Tree Training Tips" on page 105 for details on this technique). In winter, trim back the previous season's sideshoots to three buds for weak shoots or six buds for vigorous shoots. Head vigorous shoot tips back by one-quarter; prune weaker tips back by one-third. These heading cuts will encourage the formation of more side branches and fruiting spurs. Thin out crowded branches in summer to keep the center of the tree open to light and air.

On older trees, the spurs will eventually become crowded, leading to smaller, poor-quality fruit. During dormant pruning, thin out weak or crowded spurs and any that are on the undersides of branches.

Tip-bearing Apples

If left unpruned, tip-bearers tend to have upright main limbs, narrow branch angles, and many side branches. The fruit forms on the tips of the previous season's growth and little—if any—forms on the interior of the tree. 'Red Rome', 'Cortland', and 'Granny Smith' apples have this habit.

For good yields and a sturdy framework, train tip-bearers to a central leader or to an open center with three main limbs. Spread these limbs as needed to get strong branch angles. During each dormant season, stiffen the framework limbs by heading them back to within 2 feet (60 cm) of the previous heading. Thin older shoots on established trees heavily to encourage the growth of productive new fruiting wood. Don't trim the branch tips back, or you'll cut off that seasons's fruit buds.

Training to a Central Leader

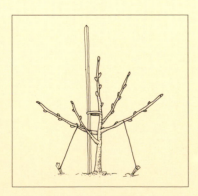

Spread or tie the branches of young trees for sturdy growth.

The next year, spread narrow branches; remove watersprouts.

On bearing plants, thin to keep the center open to light and air.

Pruning Peaches and Nectarines

Peaches and nectarines require considerable training and heavy pruning. They bear their sweet, mouth-watering fruits only on 1-year-old wood, so annual pruning is a must to encourage the production of new shoots. Although the pruning is extensive, it's not hard when you keep up with it.

Training a Young Tree

Train young peaches and nectarines to an open center shape with three or four main framework branches (see "Training to an Open Center" on page 104 for complete details on this method).

During the second spring after planting, when the new leaves are beginning to show, head the three framework branches back by about one-third of their length. Later in the growing season, pinch or rub away unwanted growth on the trunk to direct energy into those branches. Otherwise, follow the basic instructions for open center training to encourage the production of young fruiting wood.

During the training period, which may last 3 years or so, remove as little wood as possible by pruning. Instead, pinch or rub away undesirable growth as soon as possible after you see it sprout. Waiting and removing more mature shoots can sap the tree's energy and delay fruiting.

Pruning a Bearing Tree

Prune in late spring, on a dry day during or just after bloom, to avoid frost damage and disease problems. Thin out shoots that bore fruit the previous growing season by cutting back to a main or side branch. This

Peaches and nectarines need annual pruning to promote the production of young, fruit-bearing stems.

keeps the fruiting wood renewing itself. Also head back any long, weak growth by about half of its total length to keep the fruiting wood as close to the trunk and main branches as possible. (A common mistake is to let the side branches get longer and longer, which leads to weak branches that can break under the load of a good fruit crop.) If lower limbs seem to be heading toward the ground, lighten them by thinning back to a more upright branch.

In summer, thin the marble-sized fruits to 6 to 8 inches (15 to 20 cm) apart. Also thin away watersprouts or weak growth, especially in the tree's top, where they will shade out developing fruit.

If any branches seem to be strained under the weight of a heavy crop, prop them with a stout forked branch or a sturdy piece of lumber cut with a notch to cradle the branch. Consider this your signal to thin harder next year! Even if the branch doesn't break, the change of position can inhibit the growth of new wood and encourage undesirable watersprouts.

Thin developing nectarines and peaches so each fruit has plenty of room to expand and ripen completely.

Good pruning on young trees will encourage sturdy branches that can support the weight of a heavy crop.

Once pear trees begin to bear, keep pruning to a minimum; just thin out dead wood and crowded spurs.

Pruning and Training Pears

For healthy, productive pears, minimal pruning is the way to go. Make sure you give each tree plenty of room at planting time so you won't have to prune to keep it in bounds. Train young pear trees carefully, and you'll harvest succulent fruits for years with minimal work.

Train young pears to a central leader, modified central leader, open center, or espalier (see "Fruit Training and Pruning Basics" on page 102 and "Shaping Espalier" on page 150 for more information on these training styles). If you have long, wet springs that provide prime conditions for diseases like fire blight, modified central leader, open center, or espalier training may be best; these styles will provide the best possible air and light penetration to help your tree fend off infections.

Fire blight is a bacterial disease that commonly attacks pears and related plants, causing browned leaves and stems.

Training Young Pears
Young pear trees tend to have very upright growth. As you train them, spread the main branches to encourage strong branch angles and more outward, spreading growth. Each dormant season, head back the main branches at a point 30 to 36 inches (75 to 90 cm) from the previous year's heading cut. Don't head back the sideshoots.

During the growing season, make thinning cuts to remove crowded stems. If new growth is rapid and lush, pinch out shoot tips in the summer to encourage branching and compactness; otherwise, just leave the shoots unpruned. If you've chosen a modified central leader system, cut out the leader once four or five sets of branches have formed.

Pruning Bearing Pears Pears produce most of their fruit on spurs that form on 2- and 3-year-old wood. Minimal dormant pruning is best; heavy pruning will encourage lush growth that is an easy target for fire blight. Simply thin out dead wood and dense, crowded spurs. Encourage fruit set by heading unbranched shoots that are over 24 inches (60 cm) long back to about 18 inches (45 cm). Rub out or remove watersprouts whenever you see them.

Thin fruit in midsummer after some of the developing fruit has dropped off. Leave one fruit per spur.

Protect Pears from Fire Blight

Prevent fire blight by selecting resistant cultivars and keeping your tree open to air and light. Succulent, leafy growth is prone to fire blight infection, so avoid using high nitrogen fertilizers around the tree.

If fire blight does strike, you may see any or all of the following symptoms:
• Tips wilted into "shepherd's crook" shape.
• An overall "burned" look to the branch tips.
• A dark, water-soaked zone of damage progressing down a branch.
Prune infected stems back to a sideshoot or a bud on uninfected wood as soon as you see the characteristic damage. Make the cut at least 6 inches (15 cm)—and preferably 12 inches (30 cm) or more—below any visible damage. Disinfect your pruning tools by dipping or wiping the blades with isopropyl alcohol between cuts and between trees.

Blackberries bear their rich-tasting fruits on vigorous plants. Dig out unwanted suckers to keep them under control.

Fall-bearing red raspberries can form fruits on the tips of first-year canes as well as on second-year shoots.

Managing Brambles

"Brambles" is a handy, catch-all term that includes all members of the genus *Rubus:* blackberries, raspberries, loganberries, and others. These plants generally produce short-lived canes that grow one season, produce blossoms and fruit the following season, then die. Each year, new canes come up to replace the old ones.

The trick for trouble-free bramble production is regular pruning and a sturdy support system. This makes harvesting and pruning easier and keeps canes in a more productive, upright position. Generally, you'll remove fruiting canes when they're finished and tie up the younger canes to replace them.

Support Systems

A simple support system for brambles consists of a #12- to #14-gauge wire strung between two sturdy posts. Or you can set up two posts 3 feet (90 cm) apart at each end of the bed, and run parallel wires between them over the length of the bed. String the wires 3 to 4 feet (90 to 120 cm) above the ground. Make the support as long as you wish, with posts about every 15 feet (4.5 m) or so. Turnbuckles on the ends of the wires will help you to keep them taut.

If you use a training system that involves tying the canes to the wires, use raffia or string. Unlike wire ties, these natural materials will break down in the garden after you snip them off to remove old canes.

Blackberries

At planting time, shorten all blackberry canes to about 1 inch (2.5 cm) above the ground. As they grow, you can begin training them as described below.

With both thorny and thornless blackberries, be sure to remove suckers that creep out more than 6 inches (15 cm) or so on each side of the row. Don't just cut them off—several more will sprout in their place! Instead, dig the soil away from the base of each sucker until you reach the root it sprouted from. Pull the sucker off the root.

Thornless Blackberries Each summer, pinch out the tips of new thornless blackberry canes when they

In late winter, prune out weak, damaged, or diseased canes. Thin the remainder to 6 to 8 inches (15 to 20 cm) apart.

are 3 to 5 feet (90 to 150 cm) tall. Cut the fruiting canes to the ground in summer after harvest. Thin the remaining canes to leave six per plant and tie them loosely to the support wire. Before growth begins again in the spring, look for and remove any damaged or diseased canes and shorten the remaining side branches to 18 inches (45 cm).

Thorny-stemmed Blackberries Pinch the tips of new canes in summer when they reach 3 to 5 feet (90 to 150 cm) in height. Cut fruiting canes to the ground right after harvest. Thin the remaining canes to leave eight to ten canes per plant. In early spring, remove any dead, damaged, or diseased growth and all side branches that grow within 2 feet (24 inches) of the ground. Head back the remaining side branches to 12 to 16 inches (30 to 40 cm).

Red and Yellow Raspberries

At planting time, trim all newly planted raspberries down to about 1 inch (2.5 cm). The way you prune your raspberries from this point on depends on when they normally bear fruit.

Summer-bearing Red Raspberries These cultivars bear their fruits on second-year canes. In late winter, remove any weak, damaged, or diseased canes, as

A sturdy support system will help you keep brambles confined, making pruning and picking much easier!

well as any suckers that appear outside the 1-foot (30 cm) wide row. Thin the remaining canes to 6 to 8 inches (15 to 20 cm) apart and remove any winter-killed tips. Cut fruit-bearing canes to the ground after harvest; loosely tie the new canes to the support wires.

Fall-bearing (Everbearing) Red Raspberries These cultivars can bear fruit on the previous year's canes *and* on the tips of first-year canes. For one (fall) crop per year, simply cut all of the growth down to ground level in late fall or winter. For two crops per year (summer and fall), remove any weak, diseased, or damaged canes in late winter, before new growth begins. Thin the remaining canes to 6 to 8 inches (15 to 20 cm) apart and snip off the old fruit cluster at the tips. After harvesting the summer crop, remove the canes that bore fruit down to ground level. Tie the remaining canes, which will bear the fall crop, to the support wires.

Black and Purple Raspberries

Black and purple raspberries produce fruit mostly on the sideshoots on stout second-year canes. In late winter, before growth begins, cut dead, damaged, or diseased canes to the ground. Also thin out any that are less than $1/2$ inch (12 mm) in diameter. If all of the canes are smaller than this, remove all but four to six of the largest ones. Prune the side branches on the remaining stems back to 8 to 12 inches (20 to 30 cm). In summer, pinch back the new shoots to a height of 24 to 30 inches (60 to 75 cm) to encourage fullness. After harvest, cut fruited canes to the ground.

Loganberries are thought to be a hybrid between red raspberries and blackberries. Train like thornless blackberries.

Grapevines need a sturdy support and regular pruning to produce generous crops of tasty, homegrown grapes.

The vines seldom need pruning during the summer; if desired, thin dense growth to improve air circulation.

Pruning and Training Grapes

Give grapes an inch and they'll take over your garden; give them a good yearly pruning and they'll reward you with clusters of fragrant, juicy fruits.

Selecting a Support

Be sure to have some sort of support in place at planting time. The support can be as simple as a single sturdy post, if your space is limited. Training grapes on a fence, arbor, or pergola creates an attractive and productive landscape feature.

For a pretty screen or "living fence," consider a post-and-wire trellis. Supports consist of sturdy posts spaced about 24 feet (7.2 m) apart, with a line of galvanized wire (#9-, #10-, or #11-gauge) strung between them. Make the top wire about 5 feet (1.5 m) from the ground. Install turnbuckles on the ends of the wires so you can tighten them as the vines pull on them.

Basic Training

Basic training for any kind of grapes is the same from planting time until the third year. After the summer pruning in the third season after planting, your tasks will vary, depending on what kind of training system you're going to use for your grapes. The two systems discussed below—spur pruning and cane pruning—will work equally well for most kinds of grapes, although a few cultivars may be more productive under one system than another. If you want to get the highest possible yields, check with your supplier to find out which method would be best.

At Planting Time Prune away all but one cane, heading it back to two or three buds above the graft union (a swollen area near the base of the vine), if there is one. You may want to tie the resulting shoots to a temporary 4- to 6-foot (1.2 to 1.8 m) stake to keep them off the ground.

First Winter after Planting In late winter, remove all but the strongest, straightest shoot. Cut it back to two buds. This drastic cutting will encourage the young plant to produce a strong root system that can adequately support the growing vine.

During the second summer after planting, pinch off any flower clusters that form on the young grapevines.

Second Summer after Planting   Train the strongest shoot to climb the stake by tying it in at 12-inch (30 cm) intervals. Pinch the growing tip when it reaches the point where you want the horizontal arms to be. If you are going to have the vine climb on a post-and-wire trellis, pinch the vine at a point about 6 inches (15 cm) below the wire. If you're going to train the vine to grow on a wall or fence, pinch the shoot at about 3 feet (90 cm). Also pinch off any flower clusters that form.

Second Winter after Planting   In late winter, select two pencil-thick canes near the top of the trunk; these will become the horizontal arms of the branched vine. Rub off some of the buds on each cane to leave one every 4 to 5 inches (10 to 12.5 cm). Trim the tips of the canes to leave ten buds on each. Tie these canes to their support. Rub or prune off all other sideshoots from the trunk or canes.

Third Summer after Planting   The buds you left on the canes during winter pruning will become fruiting canes this growing season. Remove most of the flower clusters as they form; leave one cluster on every other shoot. Rub off any shoots that sprout from the trunk below the main canes.

Spur Pruning

This training system forms vines with permanent side arms and long-lived fruiting spurs.

Third Winter after Planting   Prune the fruiting shoots that formed on the horizontal branches back to two buds each. This should leave a two-bud spur every 4 to 5 inches (10 to 12.5 cm) along the branches. Thin out any extra spurs.

Established Vines   In late winter of each year thereafter, select a pencil-thick shoot near the base of each spur and remove all the other shoots. Cut each remaining shoot back to two buds. Continue to rub or prune off sideshoots that form along the trunk.

Each year, the vigor of your vine will help you fine-tune your pruning. If all of the shoots are thinner than a pencil, consider cutting out a few of the spurs altogether; this will encourage the plant to put all of its energy into the remaining spurs. If all of the shoots are long and thick, try leaving a few extra spurs. Select some of the new shoots on the horizontal branches and head those shoots back to two buds. This is also a good way to develop replacement spurs, since the old spurs will gradually become overgrown. Cut crowded, overgrown spurs back to the horizontal branches.

Cane Pruning

Cane pruning selects new fruit-bearing side arms every year.

Third Winter after Planting   Untie last year's horizontal branches from their supports and look for one pencil-thick cane close to the main trunk on each branch. Or, if you don't see a promising shoot on a horizontal branch, select a shoot that sprouted from the top of the trunk. Cut last year's horizontal branches back to these new shoots. Also prune out any other shoots from the trunk.

Spur-pruning Grapevines

The third summer after planting, vines will form fruiting canes.

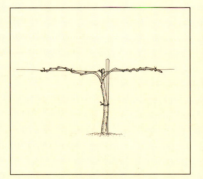

Cut each of the fruiting canes back to two buds the next winter.

If the following summer's canes are weak, cut out a few spurs.

Each winter, trim fruiting canes and a few new shoots to two buds.

Pruning vines so the fruit clusters have maximum exposure to sunlight promotes ripening and discourages diseases.

Training grapes to grow up over a metal or wooden arbor creates a feature that's both attractive and productive.

Tie the new canes to the supports and rub off the buds to leave one every 4 to 5 inches (10 to 12.5 cm). Head back the canes so each one has ten buds.

Established Vines Each year, in late winter, follow the instructions for "Third Winter after Planting" above to keep renewing the productive fruiting wood. If you notice that the previous season's shoots are thinner than a pencil, rub off a few more buds on the horizontal canes; this should promote more vigorous growth next season. If the previous season's shoots are long and thicker than a pencil, leave a few more buds than normal on the horizontal canes. If developing fruit clusters are heavily shaded by dense growth, tie back or remove a few leaves to provide more sunlight for better ripening.

For the best-quality fruit, thin developing clusters to leave room for remaining grapes to ripen fully.

Space-saving Grape Training

What can you do if you'd love to have grapes but don't have the room? Try an alternative growing system called head training.

Head training is an effective way to grow grapes in a small area, since the support is a single post. It works best in areas that don't have hot, humid summers because the crowded growth produced by head training can be more prone to disease problems.

At planting time, prune away all but one cane, heading it back to two or three buds. During winter, remove all but the strongest, straightest shoot and cut it back to two buds. Tie the vine loosely to the post and remove all but the strongest main shoot in summer.

In late winter or early spring of the following year, prune back the main shoot at a point about 3 feet (90 cm) up the post and allow it to branch out. In summer, form the "head" by cutting all of the resulting top shoots back to about 2 inches (5 cm). Make the cut right through a bud. Also remove any sideshoots below the head.

The next year, remove all but three to six of the strongest canes that grew from the head and head them back to two to four buds. Each year from this point on, remove the spurs that produced fruit the previous season.

Cherries are excellent fruit trees for the home landscape. For just a little work, you get to enjoy flowers in spring, fruit in summer, and beautiful bark in winter.

Pruning Cherries

For pies, preserves, or just plain fresh eating, it's hard to beat the fun and flavor of homegrown cherries. They're not difficult to grow and won't take up a lot of your pruning time. You won't need to thin the fruit, either.

Tart Cherries

Easy-care tart cherries (also called sour or pie cherries) are fairly compact; they grow to about 20 feet (6 m) tall if left unpruned. Pick the tangy fruit for baking or let it ripen longer on the tree until it's sweet enough for fresh eating. As a plus, tart cherries are self-fertile, so you only need one tree to get fruit.

Train young tart cherry trees to an open center system, as explained in "Fruit Training and Pruning Basics" on page 102. Work toward developing sturdy framework branches with wide crotch angles and good, even distribution on the trunk. A strong internal structure is especially important on tart cherries because they tend to be weak-wooded. Tart cherries do follow a few exceptions to the basic open center training, so keep these points in mind:

- Don't shorten the side branches or main shoot at planting time.
- During the first summer, select up to five main framework branches.
- If one branch dramatically outgrows the others during the second summer, head it back to match the others.
- Once the tree starts to bear fruit, thin out a few of the oldest branches each summer.

Sweet Cherries

Sweet cherries tend to be large trees, so make sure you allow plenty of room for each tree at planting time. Or, if space is limited, consider growing your sweet cherry as an espalier (see "Shaping Espalier" on page 150 for details). Another option is to select a genetically dwarf tree or a full-sized cherry grafted onto one of the new dwarfing root systems, such as 'GM 61'. Most sweet cherries need another cultivar for cross-pollination, although some self-fertile cultivars are available.

Train freestanding sweet cherries to a basic central leader system (as explained under "Fruit Training and Pruning Basics" on page 102), with the following exceptions:

- Don't cut back the main stem or side branches at planting time.
- When selecting the main framework limbs during the first summer, choose branches that are 12 to 15 inches (30 to 37.5 cm) apart. Prune out the rest.
- In the first winter after planting your sweet cherry tree, head the main branches back by one-third. If any of the branches are especially vigorous, head them back as much as needed to make them about the same length as the others.
- Once the tree is about 8 feet (2.4 m) tall, cut the central shoot back to a weak sideshoot each spring to encourage more side branching.
- Fruit-bearing trees need minimal pruning. Just after harvest, use thinning cuts to keep the center of the tree open to light and air. This will allow for good fruit bud formation and air circulation.

Train young cherry trees for wide branch angles and well-distributed limbs to promote sturdier mature growth.

Pruning Plums

Juicy, colorful, sun-warmed plums straight from the tree are a generous reward for good tree training and pruning. Most of the common plum trees you'll find for sale at your local nursery or garden center are either European or Japanese plums. These have different growing habits and need different kinds of pruning. Some hybrids between these two kinds are available; prune these either way.

European Plums

If left unpruned, European plums tend to have an upright habit, with narrow branch angles. They produce firm, golf-ball–sized fruits.

Train young European plums to a central leader or modified central leader system, as explained in "Fruit Training and Pruning Basics" on page 102. Spread the limbs as needed to get strong, wide branch angles that can support the weight of a heavy crop. Wait until the trees start to leaf out to do your spring pruning.

Once plants start to bear fruit, thin out a few of the longest sideshoots each summer, cutting back into the older wood. Also use thinning cuts to remove dead or damaged wood, watersprouts, and crowded growth. In early summer to midsummer, thin fruits to 1 to 3 inches (2.5 to 7.5 cm) apart.

Prune both European and Japanese plums in summer to thin out dead branches, watersprouts, and crowded growth.

Japanese Plums

Japanese plums tend to have a spreading habit and produce larger, soft fruits. They adapt well to open center training, as explained in "Fruit Training and Pruning Basics" on page 102. The first summer after planting, choose four or five well-placed main limbs and head them back to 2 to 3 feet (60 to 90 cm) to promote branching.

Once plants start to bear, thin out about one-third of the longest sideshoots each summer, cutting back into the older wood. Also use thinning cuts to remove dead wood, watersprouts, and crowded growth. In early summer to midsummer, thin fruits to 4 to 5 inches (10 to 12.5 cm) apart.

Even after thinning, you may need to prop up heavily laden plum branches to keep them from breaking in particularly good years.

After the natural fruit drop in early summer, thin remaining fruit to promote even ripening.

To keep black currant bushes vigorous and productive, thin out weak and outward-pointing growth each year.

Pruning Currants

Currants bear clusters of richly colored fruits on short, easy-to-manage bushes. The fruits are often too tart for fresh eating, but they're great in jellies and juices.

Black Currants

Black currants grow as multistemmed bushes that bear their fruit on 1- and 2-year-old wood. Get young plants off to a good start by removing all but two or three stems at planting time. Head back the remaining stems to one bud each. The following winter, cut any low-growing or spindly stems down to ground level.

Once bushes start to bear fruit, keep them productive and vigorous by removing the oldest canes each winter. Cut down all canes over 2 years old (these tend to be dark brown). Prune any spindly or outward-spreading shoots to keep the bush in an upright form. Thin out the remaining stems until you are left with six to ten of the strongest young shoots.

If plants get overgrown but otherwise look healthy, you can often rejuvenate them by cutting all the stems to just above the ground in winter. You'll lose one year's crop, but there should be plenty of fruiting wood the following year. Old black currant plants tend to be weak and may not recover well from drastic pruning; replace them instead.

Red and White Currants

Red and white currants produce their colorful fruit on short spurs on older wood and at the base of 1-year-old shoots. You can grow them as a bushy shrub at ground level or train them to a short "tree" form for more convenient harvesting and maintenance.

Shrub Training Shrub training offers the best yields, since you'll keep pruning out the old, less-productive wood.

At planting, cut all but two or three of the strongest stems to ground level. The next dormant season, cut out all but two or three of the new stems that grew up during the summer. When you are finished pruning, the plant will have two or three 2-year-old stems and two or three 1-year-old stems. Each winter thereafter, keep pruning out most of the previous summer's stems, so the plant has some 1-year-, 2-year-, and 3-year-old growth. Starting in the fourth winter after planting, cut 4-year-old stems to the ground.

"Tree" Training If you wish, you can train your red and white currants as a small bushy "tree," with a single, short trunk known as a leg. These plants may be slightly less productive, but they are attractive and easy to reach for pruning and picking.

At planting time, cut out any sideshoots growing on the bottom 4 inches (10 cm) of the main stem. Cut the remaining stems back by about half to an outward-facing bud or shoot. The following winter, head back the main stems and side branches by removing half of the previous season's growth.

On established bushes, thin out dead, diseased, or damaged wood during the dormant season. Remove suckers to keep the bottom 4 inches (10 cm) of the stem open. Head back the main shoots by half of the previous season's growth. Cut the sideshoots back to two buds.

Train white and red currants as small "trees" for easier picking or as multistemmed shrubs for better yields.

Walnuts, pecans, and hickories provide welcome shade and a useful crop. Prune them like any other mature tree.

Pruning Nut-bearing Plants

Nut-bearing trees and shrubs do double duty in the landscape, providing shade or shelter as well as an edible crop. A little regular pruning will get them off to a healthy, productive start.

Pecans, Walnuts, and Hickories

These nut trees also make wonderful shade trees in a large-scale landscape. They adapt well to the basic central leader training system discussed in "Fruit Training and Pruning Basics" on page 102. Choose well-spaced main branches that have an even spiral arrangement around the trunk.

In following years, remove dead wood anytime; do the rest of your pruning in the fall, during nut drop. Remove limbs that cross or rub and those that seem to be heading toward the center of the tree. Spread branches as needed to encourage wide, strong branch angles. As the trees begin to bear, thin lightly for good light penetration.

In areas where people or vehicles will be moving beneath your tree, raise the crown by removing a lower branch every year or two. Do this gradually—trees that are suddenly deprived of their lower limbs won't develop a strong trunk.

Handle mature nut trees the same way you would any other landscape tree, as explained in "Maintaining Mature Trees" on page 58.

Hazelnuts and Filberts

Train hazelnuts and filberts to an open center bush form with 8 to 12 main branches. During the first dormant season after planting, head the main branches back to about 2 feet (60 cm) to encourage branching.

Each winter thereafter, head back the tips and side branches by one-third. Remove any especially vigorous suckers at ground level. You may want to trim off some of the side branches that are close to the ground to make it easier to rake up dropped nuts.

Keep older plants productive by pruning a few of the oldest stems to ground level each year. Remove these stems from the center of the clump to keep the plant open to light and air circulation, thereby improving yields and decreasing the chance of disease development.

Hazelnuts and filberts are commonly grown as multistemmed bushes. Cut a few of the oldest stems to the ground each year to promote new growth.

No-prune Fruits

Some ornamental trees and shrubs provide a bonus of edible fruits. And in most cases, they'll produce a good crop without regular, intensive pruning. If you'd like to enjoy a few fruiting plants in your yard but don't want to do a lot of pruning, consider growing some of the plants discussed below.

Pawpaw

Pawpaw (*Asimina triloba*) is a native North American tree. It is at home in rich, moist soil, where it sometimes spreads by suckers in the understory of larger trees. Dark red flowers appear in spring, followed by large, drooping medium green leaves that lend a somewhat tropical effect and turn a wonderful yellow in the fall. The edible yellow-brown fruits form in fall and contain a sweet, custard-like pulp. Look for the cultivars 'Overleese', 'Taylor', and 'Taytwo' for good fruiting qualities. Prune only to remove dead wood.

Juneberry

Juneberries (*Amelanchier* spp.) have many other common names, including serviceberries, saskatoon, shadbush, and shadblow. No matter what you call them, these small trees or large shrubs make a beautiful and productive addition to any home landscape.

Juneberries bloom in early spring with many small white flowers. The berries form soon thereafter, turning red or blue-purple as they mature. The ripe berries look and taste somewhat like blueberries with almond overtones. The berries are popular with birds as well as people. If you really want to harvest all the fruit, consider covering the tree with netting. In most cases, though, there's plenty of great-tasting fruit for both you and the birds.

If desired, you can prune juneberries lightly during the dormant season to keep the tree well shaped and to remove dead wood.

Cornelian Cherry

A dogwood relative imported from Europe and Asia, cornelian cherry (*Cornus mas*) is one of the earliest spring-blooming plants. The pale yellow flowers are followed in summer by red or yellow cherry-like fruits that make great preserves. Some cultivars also produce sweeter fruits that are excellent for fresh eating. An all-season landscape plant, cornelian cherry sports red

Pawpaws make attractive landscape trees and provide sweet, pulpy fruits with little or no pruning.

fall color and peeling bark that reveals attractive gray and tan patches in the winter.

Cornelian cherries are among the most low-maintenance landscape plants, and the showy fruits are a real bonus. They are seldom bothered by insects or diseases, although birds may compete with you for the harvest. Plants rarely need pruning. If you do prune to thin out some crowded growth, wait until late winter. Bring a few of the prunings indoors and put the cut ends in a vase of water. You'll enjoy a sneak preview of spring as the cheerful flowers pop open in the indoor warmth!

After their show of yellow spring flowers, cornelian cherries offer showy fruits for fresh eating or preserving.

Malus cultivars   Rosaceae

APPLE

Late winter or early spring is a good time for most routine apple pruning. In summer, thin crowded fruits and prune as needed to remove new suckers and watersprouts.

DESCRIPTION: Standard apple trees can grow to 30 feet (9 m) and take up to 6 years to bear. Home gardeners generally prefer dwarf or semidwarf trees that grow 6–20 feet (1.8–6 m) and bear in 2–4 years. With a few self-fertile exceptions such as 'Golden Delicious', most apple trees require a compatible pollinator. Apple trees are deciduous and bear on 2-year-old and older wood; some have fruiting spurs, while others bear on the tips of branches. Zones 3–9.

WHEN TO PRUNE: In late winter or early spring before growth begins; thin fruits after "June drop."

HOW TO PRUNE: Train young trees to a central leader, as explained in "Fruit Training and Pruning Basics" on page 102. Promptly remove any sucker shoots or limbs that are dead, damaged, or dying. Following "June drop" (when some fruits naturally fall off the tree), pick or clip off some of the fruits to leave one every 6–8 inches (15–20 cm) or so. Alternatively, on spur-bearing trees you can leave one apple per spur. This results in larger, better-colored, tastier apples; it also reduces the likelihood of alternate or biennial bearing, when a tree bears just every other year. For more details on pruning apple trees, see "Training and Pruning Apple Trees" on page 106.

SPECIAL TIPS: When thinning fruits on young trees, always remove any that form on the central leader.

Prunus armeniaca   Rosaceae

APRICOT

Train apricots to an open center form to encourage good air circulation around the branches. Trim overly long branches after flowering; thin crowded fruits in early summer.

DESCRIPTION: Apricots are deciduous trees that can grow vigorously up to 30 feet (9 m) high. The attractive flowers bloom early and are often damaged by frost; provide a sheltered location. In colder climates, consider growing your apricot as an espalier against a west-facing wall. Apricots fruit on short-lived spurs that arise on the previous year's growth. Zones 5–9.

WHEN TO PRUNE: After flowering.

HOW TO PRUNE: Prune to an open center, as explained in "Fruit Training and Pruning Basics" on page 102. A vase shape with three primary leaders often works well when paired with heavy annual pruning once the tree starts bearing. Use heading cuts to reduce the length of long limbs; use thinning cuts to remove crossing, rubbing, or damaged branches. Thin the developing fruits to 2–3 inches (5–7.5 cm) apart.

Rubus spp.   Rosaceae

BLACKBERRY

Blackberries bear their succulent fruits on second-year canes. In late winter or early spring, shorten the side branches. Cut the fruit-bearing canes to the ground after harvest.

DESCRIPTION: These thorny or thornless, deciduous, suckering shrubs produce juicy fruits in midsummer on the previous year's growth. Zones 5–9.

WHEN TO PRUNE: In summer—immediately after harvest—and late winter or early spring.

HOW TO PRUNE: If you are growing thornless cultivars, cut the fruiting canes to the ground after harvest. Thin the canes to six per plant and attach them to a support wire. In spring, before growth begins, shorten the side branches to 18 inches (45 cm). Also remove any winter-damaged or diseased canes.

On thorny cultivars, cut fruiting canes to the ground immediately after harvest. Thin the remaining canes to leave eight to ten per plant. Tie those new canes loosely to a support wire. In late winter or early spring, remove any side branches that are within 2 feet (60 cm) of the ground. Trim the remaining side branches to 12–16 inches (30–40 cm). Remove any root suckers, along with any diseased or damaged growth.

SPECIAL TIPS: For more details on pruning and training blackberries and related fruits, see "Managing Brambles" on page 110.

Vaccinium spp.   Ericaceae   *Prunus* spp.   Rosaceae

BLUEBERRY   CHERRY

Blueberries don't need much pruning to produce a generous crop. In late winter or early spring, cut a few of the oldest stems to the ground each year to encourage new growth.

Prune established sweet and tart cherry trees in late spring to thin out crowded growth and to keep the center of the plants open to light and air.

DESCRIPTION: Blueberries are excellent low-maintenance plants for multiseason landscape interest.

Highbush blueberry (*V. corymbosum*): The blueberry of commerce. Has an upright, multistemmed form with spreading branches; grows to a rounded, compact 6–12 feet (1.8–3.6 m). The fruits on well-managed bushes are large and juicy. Zones 3–8.

Lowbush blueberry (*V. angustifolium*): Forms a 2-foot (60 cm) high thicket, often taking root at the branch tips. While the fruits are smaller than those of other blueberries, many find them to be tastier. Zones 2–6.

Rabbiteye blueberry (*V. ashei*): A good choice for Southern gardens. Height 10–25 feet (3–7.5 m); tolerates drought and less-acid soil better than other blueberries. The fruits are smaller and grittier than those of other blueberries. Zones 7–9.

WHEN TO PRUNE: In late winter or early spring.

HOW TO PRUNE: Young blueberries rarely need pruning. Pinch off the flowers during the first year that your blueberry blooms to ensure larger first-crop berries. On established rabbiteye and highbush blueberries—those more than 4 years old—cut a few of the oldest, weakest, or most crowded branches to ground level each year. On established lowbush blueberries, prune out up to half of the oldest stems each year.

DESCRIPTION: Cherries are deciduous trees that are ornamental as well as practical. They bloom in early spring, before the leaves expand; then they produce loads of tasty fruits in early summer. Zones 4–9; hardiness depends on the species.

Sweet cherry (*P. avium*): Height and width to 25 feet (7.5 m). It blooms and bears on spurs that grow on 2-year-old and older wood. Most cultivars are self-sterile and require a pollinator. They prefer mild, dry climates and are hardy to 20°F (-6.6°C).

Tart cherry (*P. cerasus*): Height to about 20 feet (6 m); hardy to -20°F (-28.8°C). Because they bloom and bear on year-old wood, they tend to produce much earlier than sweet cherry. Most cultivars are self-fertile, and many are known to have weak wood. Duke cherries are hybrids between sweet and tart cherries.

WHEN TO PRUNE: In late spring.

HOW TO PRUNE: Train sweet cherries to a central leader, as explained in "Fruit Training and Pruning Basics" on page 102. On young trees, head the branches back annually to develop low, spreading, easy-to-pick trees. Train tart cherries to an open center, as illustrated in "Fruit Training and Pruning Basics." On both sweet and sour cherries, begin thinning for light penetration after bearing begins. For more details, see "Pruning Cherries" on page 115.

Citrus spp.   Rutaceae

CITRUS FRUITS

Citrus trees generally need little pruning. Prune after the last spring frost to remove any dead or damaged wood. Also thin out suckers, watersprouts, and crowded growth.

DESCRIPTION: Oranges, lemons, grapefruit, and their relatives are evergreen trees or bushes with fragrant white flowers, waxy leaves, and leathery-skinned fruits. They bloom and fruit on the current season's wood any time the weather is favorable. Plants may have thorns. Zones 9–10.

WHEN TO PRUNE: In early spring, when the danger of frost—if any—is over.

HOW TO PRUNE: Shorten the main branches on newly planted trees by one-third to encourage sideshoots. Train oranges and grapefruits to a central leader, as explained in "Fruit Training and Pruning Basics" on page 102. Lemons are more open and rangy, so pinch or head back stems as needed for compactness. Use thinning cuts on any young citrus to let light and air into the center of the tree. Avoid removing the lower limbs, as they normally produce the most fruit. Once a tree starts bearing, prune only to remove diseased, dying, or dead branches. Remove suckers and watersprouts (vigorous, upright shoots).

SPECIAL TIPS: If you can stand to be without a crop for 2 years or so, you can usually rejuvenate an overgrown citrus tree by pruning the top back hard to the main branches. Spreading some organic fertilizer around the base of the tree can help it recover more quickly.

Ribes spp.   Grossulariaceae

CURRANT

Red and white currants are usually trained to grow as open, cup-shaped bushes on a short main stem. Black currants are commonly grown as many-stemmed shrubs.

DESCRIPTION: Currants are deciduous shrubs with an upright or spreading habit; they can reach 3–7 feet (90–210 cm) high and wide. Currants are grown for the $^1/_4$–$^3/_4$-inch (6–18 mm) fruits that form on year-old and older wood. The plants prefer full sun and well-drained, loamy soil. Zones 3–7.

WHEN TO PRUNE: In late winter or early spring before growth begins.

HOW TO PRUNE: At planting time, trim black currant by cutting out all but two or three canes; head each of these remaining canes back to one bud. Thereafter, annually remove all canes over 2 years old, and thin out the rest until you are left with six to ten of the strongest canes.

For shrubby red or white currants, cut all but two or three of the strongest stems to the ground at planting. Each year for the next 2 years, cut out most of the youngest stems. Starting in the fourth year, also cut out the 4-year-old stems.

If your plant is growing on a single stem, cut out any sideshoots growing from the bottom 4 inches (10 cm) of the main stem at planting time. Also trim the remaining sideshoots back by half. In following seasons, trim the main shoots by removing half of the previous season's growth. Cut sideshoots back to two buds. Remove suckers.

SPECIAL TIPS: For more details, see "Pruning Currants" on page 117.

Sambucus spp.   Caprifoliaceae

ELDERBERRY

Prune elderberries during the dormant season to remove any dead canes. Also cut one-third of the oldest stems to the ground each year. Pull or clip suckers to keep plants in bounds.

DESCRIPTION: Elderberries are multistemmed deciduous shrubs that are broad and rounded in outline, with spreading, arching branches. They bloom and fruit on the previous year's wood and prefer full sun and a deep, moist, humus-rich soil. Give them plenty of room—they creep outward by suckers—and a thick layer of mulch. Elderberries are self-pollinating but are more productive if you grow two or more cultivars near each other.

American elderberry (*S. canadensis*): Height 6–12 feet (1.8–3.6 m). Large, flat-topped clusters of white flowers in summer, followed by purple-black fruits. 'Adams' is an early-ripening cultivar with medium-sized berries. Zones 3–9.

European elderberry (*S. nigra*): Height 10–30 feet (3–9 m), with large clusters of yellowish white flowers in June, followed by shiny black berries in September. Zones 5–8.

WHEN TO PRUNE: During the dormant season.

HOW TO PRUNE: Remove one-third of the oldest stems each year.

SPECIAL TIPS: Some cultivars of European elderberry are grown for their foliage rather than their fruit. 'Aurea' has golden new foliage; 'Marginata' has green leaves edged with white. To encourage strong new shoots and good leaf production, cut these types to the ground or to a low framework in early spring.

Ficus carica   Moraceae

FIG

Fig trees produce good crops with light thinning and trimming. On bush forms, prune out some of the oldest growth each year and head back the rest. Remove suckers as they appear.

DESCRIPTION: These exotic-looking small trees or large shrubs bear large, three- to five-lobed, dark green leaves that are evergreen south of Zone 8. Plants can grow 10–15 feet (3–4.5 m) tall. Figs normally bear fruit on the previous year's wood; in warmer climates, a second crop will grow on the current season's wood as well. Select a self-pollinating cultivar that's known to perform in your climate. Figs are normally hardy in Zones 8–10, but they can grow and produce well in more northern climates with winter protection.

WHEN TO PRUNE: In late winter or early spring before growth begins.

HOW TO PRUNE: You can train figs in a bush or tree form; bush forms are generally easier to protect in cool climates. Each year, cut one-third of the oldest growth to ground level and trim the remaining shoots back to 2–3 feet (60–90 cm). Or train a tree form to multiple leaders, removing suckers and basal sprouts annually. Use thinning cuts to control the size and heading cuts to stimulate new fruiting branches.

Corylus spp.   Betulaceae

FILBERT

Most filberts grow as many-stemmed shrubs. Trim shoot tips and side branches each year in late winter or early spring. On established plants, also prune out one-third of the oldest stems.

DESCRIPTION: Filberts, also called hazelnuts, are deciduous large shrubs or small trees grown for their tasty nuts. All bear their nuts on the previous year's growth. Plant in deep, loamy soil and full sun to partial shade.

American filbert (*C. americana*): Multiple-stemmed shrub with a rounded form; height 10–15 feet (3–4.5 m). Zones 3–8.

European hazel or filbert (*C. avellana*): Rounded shrub; height 12–20 feet (3.6–6 m). Zones 4–8.

WHEN TO PRUNE: In late winter or early spring before growth begins.

HOW TO PRUNE: Train the bushes to an open center for easy harvest. Remove any particularly vigorous suckers. Head back shoot tips and side branches by a third each year. Rejuvenate older plants by removing one-third of the oldest stems each year; take these stems from the center to keep the shrub open to light and air. Head back tops and laterals. For more pruning and training tips, see "Hazelnuts and Filberts" on page 118.

SPECIAL TIPS: *C. avellana* 'Contorta', commonly known as Harry Lauder's walking stick or corkscrew hazel, is grown primarily for its curiously twisted stems. These plants are generally grafted onto the roots of the species, which are prone to suckering. Remove suckers regularly to keep them from spoiling the unique branching structure of this cultivar.

Ribes spp.   Grossulariaceae

GOOSEBERRY

During the dormant season, prune old, unproductive gooseberry stems to the ground. In summer, trim side branches back to three to five leaves. Thin stems as needed for easy picking.

DESCRIPTION: Gooseberries are deciduous shrubs that grow 3–6 feet (90–180 cm) high and wide. Their stems are armed with long, sharp spines. Gooseberries are grown for the yellow, green, orange, pink, red, purple, or black berries that grow on shoots 1 year old and older. Plant in a protected, sunny site and give them plenty of mulch. They are best suited for cool climates. Zones 3–6.

WHEN TO PRUNE: In late winter or early spring before growth begins and again in summer.

HOW TO PRUNE: Train gooseberries to a spreading bush form. At planting time, thin out all but the strongest shoots by cutting them at ground level; leave no more than six stems. On established plants, remove any unproductive canes—usually those over 3 years old—during the dormant season. In summer, trim the side branches to three to five leaves. Use gloves to work with these well-armed plants!

SPECIAL TIPS: The culture of gooseberries and other member of the genus *Ribes* was restricted for many years, as these plants were thought to all be alternate hosts for a disease called white pine blister rust. It's now known that gooseberries are generally resistant to the disease. Although the Federal ban was lifted in the 1960s, check with your local extension agent to find out if any local laws still apply before you plant.

Vitis spp.   Vitaceae

GRAPE

There are many ways to train and prune grapevines, but they are generally based on one of two techniques: spur pruning or cane pruning. Either works well for most grapes.

DESCRIPTION: Grapes are deciduous vines grown for their clusters of juicy berries. They fruit on the current season's wood arising from year-old canes. For good growth, choose a sunny site away from frost pockets and begin preparing the site well ahead of planting. Most grapevines can live for many years, so the time you invest in preparing a good site will be time well spent. Zones 4–10.

WHEN TO PRUNE: In late winter or early spring before growth begins and again in summer.

HOW TO PRUNE: There are many ways in which to train and prune grapes. Begin by pruning each plant to one stem, then pruning that stem back to two or three live buds. Also set in a support stake at planting time. The following winter, select the strongest, straightest shoot, and cut it back to two buds, removing the other shoots. Also remove root suckers. Train the new shoot up the stake, and pinch the top when it reaches the height you want. The following winter, select two pencil-thick canes at the top. Rub off some of the buds on each cane to leave one every 4–5 inches (10–12.5 cm). Trim the tips of the canes to leave ten buds on each. Tie these canes to their support. Rub or prune off all other sideshoots from the trunk or canes.

At this point, you can follow either a spur pruning or a cane pruning system; see "Pruning and Training Grapes" on page 112 for details.

Carya spp.   Juglandaceae

HICKORY

Hickories grow to be tall trees that provide some shade as well as an edible crop. Prune young trees in fall to promote a strong main trunk and sturdy side branches.

DESCRIPTION: These large, long-lived trees can grow to a height of 60 feet (18 m) or more. The nuts grow inside thick husks and drop in fall.
Shagbark hickory (*C. ovata*): Has a distinctive ash gray peeling bark, yellow fall color, and sweet nuts. Zones 4–8.
Shellbark hickory (*C. laciniosa*): Tends to grow slightly shorter than shagbark hickory; also has very sweet nuts. Zones 5–8.

WHEN TO PRUNE: In fall, at nut drop.

HOW TO PRUNE: Train young trees to a central leader, thinning out dead, dying, crossing, or rubbing limbs. Also prune out limbs that emerge at a narrow angle (less than 45 degrees) from the trunk. Remove the lower limbs gradually—over a period of several years—to provide headroom for walking and mowing beneath the tree.

SPECIAL TIPS: Hickories make tall, stately shade trees, but their dropping leaves and nuts can be a maintenance problem. You'll also want to plant at least two for cross-pollination, unless there are many other hickories growing in your area. If you have a small yard, hickories are probably not a good choice for you.

Actinidia spp.   Actinidiaceae

KIWI

Kiwi vines will often produce some fruits with little or no pruning, but careful training and regular trimming through the year can reward you with a generous harvest.

DESCRIPTION: These deciduous twining vines produce sweet fruits. Most kiwis require cross-pollination; plant one male for every three or four female vines. Kiwis grow best in full sun or partial shade and in evenly moist but well-drained soil. Chinese kiwi (*A. deliciosa*): The kiwi of commerce. A rampant grower to 30 feet (9 m). Zones 7–10. Hardy kiwi (*A. arguta*): Also a rampant grower; height 20–30 feet (6–9 m). Zones 3–8.

WHEN TO PRUNE: In midwinter and through the growing season as needed.

HOW TO PRUNE: Insert a stake next to the vine at planting time. Cut out all but one stem. Remove any sideshoots from the remaining stem and train it up the stake. When the stem reaches the height where you want the horizontal arms to be, pinch out the tip to promote sideshoots. Train one shoot in each direction; remove the others. For the first few years, trim these "arms" back each winter, leaving about 2 feet (60 cm) of the previous season's growth to encourage fruiting canes. Thin the fruiting canes to 1 foot (30 cm) apart.

On mature plants, cut the arms back to about 7 feet (2.1 m) each winter. Cut out 3-year-old fruiting canes. Head the sideshoots on remaining canes back to seven or eight buds. During the summer, trim very vigorous canes to four or five buds.

Olea europa   Oleaceae

OLIVE

Thin established olive trees in late winter or early spring to promote the production of new fruiting wood. Thin crowded fruits to encourage an equally good crop next year.

DESCRIPTION: These evergreen trees can grow to a height of 30–40 feet (9–12 m). They bear scaly, silver-green leaves, fragrant flowers, and 1¹/₂-inch (37 mm) green to glossy black fruits on the previous year's wood. Zones 9–10.

WHEN TO PRUNE: In late winter or early spring before growth begins.

HOW TO PRUNE: Train young plants to an open center form, as explained in "Fruit Training and Pruning Basics" on page 102. Trim bearing trees lightly for shape. For the best harvest, thin out wood that has fruited. Thinning the fruits can also help ensure a good crop each year, instead of every other year; remove some of the developing fruits to leave three to five olives per 1 foot (30 cm) of branch.

Prunus persica Rosaceae	*Pyrus communis* Rosaceae

PEACH

PEAR

Training peaches to an open-center system allows for good air circulation and easy harvesting. Thin out older shoots heavily in late spring, and head back any overly long branches.

Holding pruning to a minimum will help to keep your pear trees healthy. Spread branches of young trees to encourage a sturdy framework. Thin out suckers and watersprouts as you see them.

DESCRIPTION: Peaches are broad-spreading, deciduous trees that grow 15–25 feet (4.5–7.5 m) high. They have long, thin, lance-shaped leaves, pink flowers in early spring, and fuzzy, sweet, yellow- or white-fleshed fruits that form on the previous season's wood. Most peaches are self-fertile, so you only need to plant one to get a crop. Plant in full sun and well-drained soil. Zones 5–9.

WHEN TO PRUNE: In late spring in dry weather, during or just after bloom.

HOW TO PRUNE: Peaches call for severe pruning more than any other fruit tree. Train peaches to an open center form, as explained in "Fruit Training and Pruning Basics" on page 102. When the tree is young, select three or four main branches that are spaced no less than 8 inches (20 cm) apart on the main trunk. The second spring after planting, head those main branches back by about one-third of their length to outward-growing sideshoots. Once your tree is bearing, prune heavily. Thin out shoots that bore fruit the previous season. Head back long shoots by about half of their total length. Thin fruits when they are about the size of marbles to about 4–8 inches (10–20 cm) apart. The rule of thumb is the earlier the cultivar, the wider the thinning. For more details, see "Pruning Peaches and Nectarines" on page 108.

DESCRIPTION: These spreading or upright deciduous trees have glossy green leaves and white blossoms. Pears bear fruit on long-lived spurs; they require cross-pollination to produce a good crop. They prefer full sun and a neutral soil. Although they can tolerate imperfect drainage, they are sensitive to drought. Zones 4–9.

WHEN TO PRUNE: In the late dormant season.

HOW TO PRUNE: Avoid heavy pruning on young trees or you'll delay bearing. Train European pears to a central leader and Asian pears to an open center; both of these systems are explained in "Fruit Training and Pruning Basics" on page 102. If the tree is very upright, consider spreading the branches to encourage outward growth and stronger branch angles. On bearing trees, thin out dead wood and crowded spurs. Head back long, unbranched shoots to about 18 inches (45 cm). Thin fruits in midsummer to leave one per spur. For more details, see "Pruning and Training Pears" on page 109.

SPECIAL TIPS: Open center training improves air circulation and light penetration, helping pear trees to resist the damaging disease fire blight. If fire blight becomes a problem—causing wilted or burned-looking branch tips—prune out the damaged wood, along with at least 6 inches (15 cm) of healthy wood. Dip or wipe your pruners with isopropyl alcohol between cuts.

Carya illinoinensis   Juglandaceae

PECAN

Prune young pecan trees in fall to develop sturdy branches and to remove rubbing or crossing limbs. On established trees, gradually prune off lower branches if they're in your way.

DESCRIPTION: Pecans are tall, broad-spreading trees growing 70–100 feet (21–30 m) high and 40–75 feet (12–2.5 m) wide. Although pecans are monoecious (having male and female flowers on the same plant), the male flowers on a given tree bloom ahead of the female flowers; for this reason, it's best to have multiple trees for a good nut crop. Pecans release a lot of pollen, and if there are many trees, everything around will be covered with a yellow sheen. Pecans bear on long-lived spurs. The nuts grow in husks that stay on the tree for a time after the nuts fall. Zones 6–9.

WHEN TO PRUNE: In fall, during nut drop.

HOW TO PRUNE: Train young pecans to a central leader, as explained in "Fruit Training and Pruning Basics" on page 102. Prune lightly for the first 5 to 6 years; cut out or spread branches growing at a narrow (less than 45 degree) angle, and eliminate crossing or rubbing limbs. If you need headroom to get under the tree, gradually remove the lower limbs over a period of several years. Mature pecans need little pruning, except for the removal of dead wood.

Diospyros spp.   Ebenaceae

PERSIMMON

In late winter or early spring, prune young persimmons to remove suckers and limbs that cross, rub, or grow from the trunk at a narrow angle. Thin older trees annually for best yields.

DESCRIPTION: Persimmons are deciduous trees that bear orange fall fruits on the current season's wood. Fall color on these plants usually includes stunning reds and oranges. Some persimmons need cross-pollination for good fruit set.

Asian persimmon (*D. kaki*): Low-branched, wide-spreading tree with white flowers in late spring. The 2–3-inch (5–7.5 cm) long fruits usually have a waxy bloom. Height to 30 feet (9 m); some dwarf cultivars are available. Zones 7–10.

Common persimmon (*D. virginiana*): More upright; can become a handsome shade tree. Height 35–60 feet (10.5–18 m). The fruits are about 1 inch (2.5 cm) wide, with a white, waxy bloom. Zones 5–10.

WHEN TO PRUNE: In late winter or early spring before growth begins.

HOW TO PRUNE: Train to a central leader, as explained in "Fruit Training and Pruning Basics" on page 102. Choose five or six main limbs that are well spaced along the trunk. Remove crossing or rubbing branches, basal suckers, and branches that join the trunk at a narrow angle (less than 45 degrees). Plants needs little else until they mature; then thin annually for light penetration and to stimulate bearing.

PLUM

QUINCE

Train upright growing plums—mostly the European types—to a central leader system. Spreading plums—including most of the Japanese types—adapt better to open-center training.

Thin established quinces each year during the dormant season to keep the center of the plant open to light and air. Remove any suckers as they appear.

DESCRIPTION: Plums are deciduous trees that produce plump, sweet fruits. They bloom on long-lived spurs that grow on year-old and older wood. The flowers appear before or with the leaves; greenish, yellow, red, purple, or blue fruits develop through the summer.

European plum (*P. domestica*): Has an upright habit and firm fruits. Zones 5–8.

Japanese plum (*P. salicina*): Spreading habit; large, soft fruits. Zones 6–10.

WHEN TO PRUNE: In late spring.

HOW TO PRUNE: Train European plums to a central leader or modified central leader, as explained in "Fruit Training and Pruning Basics" on page 102. Once the tree is bearing, thin out a few of the longest sideshoots each summer to lighten branch ends and prevent breakage. Train Japanese plums to an open center form; head the main limbs back to promote branching. Once the tree is bearing, thin to improve light and air penetration. On both species, thin fruits to leave one every 4–5 inches (10–12.5 cm).

DESCRIPTION: Quinces bear yellow, roughly rounded fruits that are inedible raw but tasty when cooked into jelly or added to apple pie. The plants grow 10–15 feet (3–4.5 m) high and can be trained as bushes, trees, or espalier. The large, deciduous green leaves have silvery undersides, and the pale pink flowers bloom in spring. Quinces fruit on the tips of the current season's growth. Zones 5–9.

WHEN TO PRUNE: During the dormant season.

HOW TO PRUNE: Train shrub- and tree-form quinces to an open center, as explained in "Fruit Training and Pruning Basics" on page 102. Thin bearing plants to improve light penetration. Avoid making heading cuts, as quinces bear on the branch tips. For information on training espaliers, see "Shaping Espalier" on page 150.

Rubus spp.   Rosaceae

RASPBERRY

When and how you prune your raspberry plants depends on where they bear their fruits. Whatever system you use, wear gloves and long sleeves to protect yourself from the thorns!

DESCRIPTION: These brambles have thorny stems and tasty fruits. Zones 3–8.

WHEN TO PRUNE: In late winter and after harvest.

HOW TO PRUNE:

BLACK OR PURPLE RASPBERRIES: Before growth begins, remove all canes less than ¹/₂ inch (12 mm) in diameter. If all canes are smaller than this, remove all but four to six of the largest ones. Also remove weak, diseased, or insect-damaged canes. Prune all side branches to 8–12 inches (20–30 cm). In summer, pinch back the shoots to a height of 24–30 inches (60–75 cm). After harvest, cut fruited canes to the ground.

FALL-BEARING RED AND YELLOW RASPBERRIES: For one (fall) crop each year, cut down all canes in late fall or winter. For two smaller crops per year, remove any weak, diseased, or insect-damaged canes before growth begins. Thin remaining canes to 6–8 inches (15 to 20 cm) apart. Snip off the old fruit clusters at the tips. After the summer harvest, cut down the old canes.

SUMMER-BEARING RED RASPBERRIES: Before growth begins, remove weak, diseased, or insect-damaged canes. Thin canes 6–8 inches (15–20 cm) apart in a row and remove winterkilled tips. After harvest, cut down all canes that bore fruit.

SPECIAL TIPS: For more details on pruning raspberries, see "Managing Brambles" on page 110.

Juglans spp.   Juglandaceae

WALNUT

Prune young walnuts in fall to promote a sturdy branch structure. On older trees, gradually remove the lowest limbs if you need room to walk or work beneath them.

DESCRIPTION: Walnuts are deciduous nut trees that perform best in full sun and deep, moist, well-drained soil. In the garden and landscape, they can have an inhibiting effect on other plants. Use them in large-scale situations where you can plant them alone or grouped with other walnuts.

Black walnut (*J. nigra*): Has a clear, straight trunk and an upright oval crown; height 50–75 feet (15–22.5 m). Seeds are cloaked in thick green husks and begin to drop in the fall. Zones 5–7.

English or Persian walnut (*J. regia*): Similar to black walnut, but more squat and rounded in outline; height 40–60 feet (12–18 m). The nut separates more easily from the husk. Zones 6–8. The Carpathian walnut, grown from a seed source found in the Carpathian Mountains, is useful to Zone 5.

WHEN TO PRUNE: In fall, during nut drop.

HOW TO PRUNE: Prune young trees to a central leader, as explained in "Fruit Training and Pruning Basics" on page 102. Select four to six evenly spaced main branches. Prune out crossing or rubbing branches, along with those that join the main trunk at a narrow angle (less than 45 degrees). Thin older trees for light penetration. If you need headroom to walk or mow under the tree, gradually remove the lower branches over a period of several years.

PRUNING ROSES, FLOWERS, AND HERBS

All gardeners know that a landscape brimming with flowers doesn't just happen. Abundant, beautiful blooms are the result of careful plant selection, proper planting, and conscientious care through the seasons. When you follow through with judicious pruning, pinching, and training, your plants are in prime condition to thrive and flower generously.

Just like other shrubs, roses respond to good pruning with good growth. And though it may seem strange to think of pruning geraniums or basil as you would trees and shrubs, annuals, perennials, and herbs also respond to the same basic kinds of cuts with strong, healthy shoots. These vigorous plants will provide the colorful flowers and foliage that light up your landscape from spring through fall. Simple techniques like deadheading make it easy to keep plants looking good and possibly even flowering longer.

Pruning also helps to reduce insect and disease problems by opening roses and other bushy plants to light and air. Dense, crowded growth will shelter pests like aphids from driving rains and soap sprays, leading to pest population explosions. While appropriate pruning won't completely eliminate these pests, it will help to discourage them. Plants prone to fungal diseases will similarly benefit from good pruning that exposes more growth to light and air.

Along with judicious pruning, a little careful training can give your garden a tidy, well-maintained look. No one says you have to spend hours laboriously staking each stem until your plants stand stiff in rows like toy soldiers. But a few minutes spent supporting particular plants can make the difference between clean, easy-to-see blooms and sprawling stems that drop their flowers face first into the mud.

Savvy pruning and training may sound like a lot of work, but they don't have to be. This chapter will guide you through the basics of pruning hybrid tea roses, shrub roses, climbers, miniatures, and many other forms of these landscape gems. You'll also learn how to trim and train a wide variety of annuals, perennials, and herbs to encourage flowers or foliage and strong, self-supporting stems. And you'll find out about staking techniques that help tall flowers stay straight and beautiful with minimal fuss.

For their stunning flowers and fabulous fragrance, roses are among the best loved landscape plants. Careful routine pruning is a key part of keeping your roses looking their best and blooming generously.

Rose Pruning Basics

Well-timed, careful pruning helps to keep roses healthy, vigorous, and free-blooming. Although the specific recommendations for different types of roses vary, there are some basic techniques that apply to all. For instance, you'll always start pruning any rose by removing dead, damaged, diseased, thin, weak, or crossing branches. Deadheading and removing blind shoots (those with no flower buds) are also common pruning tasks on certain types of roses. Of course, you'll want to harvest some of those roses for your indoor enjoyment; that's pruning, too!

Tools and Supplies

A good pair of bypass (scissor-style) pruners and loppers are all you need to do most rose pruning. For renovation, or for large bush roses, you may also need a pruning saw. If you know that your plants are infected with a disease like canker or crown gall, plan on disinfecting your tools by dipping or wiping the blades with isopropyl alcohol between cuts or at least between plants.

Painting pruning cuts with wood glue can help prevent borers from entering the stems. For small jobs, apply the glue right out of the bottle or tube; for large jobs, dab on the glue—from a can—with a small brush.

Finally, protect your hands and arms from thorns (and from your pruners!) with a good pair of gloves. Long gauntlet-style gloves are especially useful for rose pruning, since they shield both your hands and your forearms. Long sleeves and pants can also help prevent nicks and scratches from errant thorny canes.

When to Prune

Good pruning starts at planting time. If you're planting a rose from bareroot stock, first look carefully at the roots. Healthy roots are normally light-colored, firm, and fibrous. Prune away any roots that are broken, dried, dead, or rotten. Trim healthy roots only if you must. Try not to prune healthy roots just because they won't fit into the hole that you've dug; first consider enlarging the hole. Spread the roots out over a cone of soil in the hole, then fill the rest of the hole with soil, and water well.

Pick Up Your Prunings!

Keeping the garden clean is your first defense against rose diseases. Many common diseases, including black spot and rust, perpetuate themselves on the foliage—whether or not it's attached to the plant. Don't just leave prunings where they fall; burn them or bury them if you can to prevent the spread of disease-causing pathogens. Fall cleanup of dropped leaves is important for the same reason. Some rose growers trim off any foliage that persists on the stems into the fall.

Long pants, long sleeves, and a sturdy pair of gloves can make rose pruning as painless as possible for you!

Careful pruning at planting and each year thereafter will encourage your roses to bloom freely.

Late winter or early spring is the best time to prune established roses for showy summer flower displays.

Removing faded flowers can encourage new flowering growth, but stop by late summer to avoid winter damage.

On container-grown stock, remove the pot and loosen any circling roots. Put the root ball in the hole, backfill with soil, and water the plant well.

Once your bareroot or container-grown rose is in the ground, remove any dead, damaged, or weak twigs. Be sure to cut back into good wood and to buds pointing in directions where you want the new growth to go.

On established roses, late winter or early spring is generally the best time for major pruning. Swelling growth buds on the canes is a good sign that the time is right. During the season, remove any dead or dying stems as you see them. If you are not growing a rose for its showy fruit (hips), cut off the flowers as they fade. This kind of pruning will encourage new growth, though, so

Pruning off developing fruits can encourage your rose plant to produce more flowers.

stop deadheading by late summer. Otherwise, the new growth may not have time to harden before cold weather sets in, and it may get killed or damaged by the first winter freezes.

How to Prune

Start any rose pruning session by removing any dead or diseased stems. If you need to remove a whole stem, cut it to the ground or graft union; otherwise, just trim back into good wood at least

1 inch (2.5 cm) below where any damage is evident.

If the center, or pith, of the stem is still dark or discolored at that point, cut the cane back farther until the pith is white. Look for and remove any weak or spindly stems that are much thinner than the others. If you see any canes that cross or rub, remove one of the two. Make each cut about 1/4 inch (6 mm) above a bud, at a 45 degree angle away from the bud. In most cases, you'll want to cut to a bud that faces away from the center of the plant to encourage outward growth and good air circulation. If you want to promote more upright growth on a spreading rose, you may choose to prune to an inner, upward-pointing bud. Dispose of the remaining debris as explained in "Pick Up Your Prunings!".

Pruning to outward-facing canes will keep the center of the plant open to good air circulation and discourage diseases.

Sucker Removal

Most modern roses are budded onto more-vigorous species-rose rootstocks, so you'll want to control any sucker growth that you see coming from the roots. Growth from these suckers is often stronger than the top growth (what you actually bought the rose for). If left unchecked, suckers can quickly crowd out the more desirable growth.

Pull suckers off where they join the roots—don't just cut them at ground level.

To properly remove a sucker, scrape the soil away from its base, and snap it off where it joins the rootstock. This technique removes any dormant buds that might be present at the point where the sucker joins the root. Don't simply cut the sucker off at ground level, because more sucker shoots will probably arise for you to deal with later.

Rose Renovation

If you are faced with an overgrown bush or climbing rose, renovation may be in order. Removing the old stems will encourage strong new growth and better flowering. Early spring, when the buds begin to swell, is a great time to reclaim a neglected rose. Choose one of the two approaches outlined here. Mature rose stems can be especially thorny and vicious, so heavy gloves and sturdy clothing are a necessity. Also choose your strongest tools—lopping shears and a pruning saw will likely be more useful than your hand-held shears.

If your rose bears flowers in clusters, snip the center flower when it's spent or wait until the whole cluster is done.

One-step Method The one-step method is drastic but fast. Simply cut all of the top growth to just above the ground or to the graft union, if there is one. (If you're renovating a climbing rose, it may be easier to first unfasten the top growth from the supports and lay it on the ground before you cut.) The next spring, begin to prune and train the regrowth as you would on a young plant. Plants should begin to bloom again the following year, if not sooner.

Two-step Method This approach is a little more involved, but it may keep you from losing a whole season of bloom. Prune out the oldest stems at the base, leaving three to five of the younger canes. Trim these canes back by a quarter to a third to shape the plant and encourage new growth. If the rose is a climber, fasten the canes back onto the supports.

Over time, roses trained to climb structures can put on lots of crowded growth. Take down the stems every few years, and cut out the oldest wood to keep plants healthy.

Hybrid teas and similar roses need pruning to develop an open-centered plant with strong growth from the base.

Pruning Common Garden Roses

Hybrid teas, floribundas, and other bush roses require annual pruning to keep them vigorous, disease-resistant, and well shaped. Wait to do your spring pruning until cold weather has ended and the stem buds on your roses begin to swell. If you prune too soon, freezing weather may cause additional damage, and you'll have to prune again later.

Hybrid Teas and Grandifloras

Moderate to heavy pruning in spring, followed by lighter trimming in summer and fall, will keep these plants producing beautiful blooms to brighten your garden or your indoor arrangements.

Most hybrid teas, grandifloras, and floribundas bloom on new growth, so they need moderate to heavy pruning.

Spring Pruning Remove any canes that have been killed by cold, disease, or insects, making your cut at the graft union. Also remove any suckers that arise from below the graft.

The next step is to prune away all but three to six of the most robust young canes by cutting them off at the base. Remove branches that point inward or cross and any growth that is weak or spindly. To encourage large, long-stemmed flowers, cut the remaining canes to 15 to 18 inches (37.5 to 45 cm) above the ground. For smaller but more abundant flowers, prune lightly: Remove tip growth to a bud 1 inch (2.5 cm) or more below the lowest dead or damaged wood. Cut to an outside bud unless you have a spreading rose, such as 'Crimson Glory,' that you want to grow more upright.

Summer Pruning Throughout the growing season, remove any blind (non-flowering) shoots or weak growth. Rub off any buds that are pointing toward the center of the plant.

Disbudding for Bigger Blooms

Disbudding is a pruning method that produces fewer but larger flowers. It is most commonly used for hybrid tea roses. Choose a stem with a big terminal flower bud, and gently rub or break off the small side buds below it. This will direct the plant's energy into just one large flower for that stem.

Other than that, you'll take care of most of the summer pruning when you cut the flowers to bring indoors. During the first few years, resist the temptation to cut long-stemmed roses; the loss of all that growth really saps the energy of a young plant. Cut the flowers with a short stem instead, leaving as many leaves as possible. On older plants, it's okay to take longer stems—just be sure to make a proper, slanted cut $\frac{1}{4}$ inch (6 mm) above a bud.

When cutting fresh flowers or removing faded ones, make your cut just above the highest five-leaflet leaf on the stem. If there are no five-leaflet leaves, cut to just above the first strong, well-placed bud below the bloom. As the season winds down in late summer, leave some flowers on the plant to let some rose hips form. This signals the plant to slow down, discouraging new growth that would be damaged by cold weather and encouraging the existing growth to harden off.

When cutting fresh flowers or removing dead ones, make cuts just above an outward-facing five-leaflet leaf.

Fall Pruning If you live in an area with particularly cold and windy winters, shorten the canes by one-third to one-half in mid- to late-fall. This will help to keep the wind from whipping the long canes around and loosening the roots. Wait until spring, after the chance of severe cold weather, to finish pruning the canes to the recommended height.

Floribundas and Polyanthas

Floribunda and polyantha roses tend to form bushier plants with many clusters of small flowers. Moderate to light pruning will keep the plants well shaped and encourage good flowering.

Spring Pruning In spring, remove dead, diseased, crossing, congested, or weak canes by cutting them off at the graft union. Keep six to eight vigorous canes. Cut these back to 18 to 24 inches (45 to 60 cm) for hard pruning or to the first bud that's 1 inch (2.5 cm) or more below any damage for light pruning. (Hard pruning encourages later flowering and new growth from the base of the plant. Light pruning allows for earlier flowering and is generally the best approach for polyanthas.)

Summer Pruning Through the growing season, remove weak or inward-growing branches, keeping the plant open to light and air. Cut the clusters of flowers or faded blooms to just above the first strong, well-placed bud. In late summer, stop deadheading and let some rose hips form to encourage any new growth to harden off before cold weather arrives.

Fall Pruning In cold-winter areas, you may want to cut the canes back lightly (by about one-quarter) in mid- to late-fall to reduce the chance of winter damage. Or simply wait until spring and prune any damaged growth as needed.

Standard or Tree Roses

Standard or tree roses are usually hybrid tea, grandiflora, or floribunda roses grafted onto the stiff trunks of wild climbing roses. Stiff as they are, the trunks normally cannot support that heavy top growth without help, so plan on keeping them staked for life.

Regular annual trimming encourages lots of flowers. In early spring, cut the top shoots back to 6 to 8 inches (15 to 20 cm) from the trunk. Leave at least one or two buds on hybrid tea shoots and four to six buds on floribunda or grandiflora shoots. Also remove any sprouts that arise along the trunk below the graft union.

Keep miniature roses vigorous and free-blooming by removing the oldest stems each spring; then trim to shape.

Large-flowered climbers bloom on side branches on 2- to 3-year canes. Shorten these side branches in spring.

Pruning Climbing Roses

Climbing roses add a touch of elegance to any landscape. With a bit of routine pruning and training, their long, thorny canes can clamber up and over fences, arbors, trellises, or other sturdy structures to produce masses of beautiful summer blooms. For tips on reclaiming old, overgrown climbers, see "Rose Renovation" on page 136.

Large-flowered Climbers

Many of the climbing roses you'll find for sale at the garden center bear large flowers on fairly stiff canes. Train these beauties to climb a trellis or other support by attaching the canes loosely with a figure-eight tie (as explained in "Attaching Vines to Supports" on page 87). Large-flowered climbers seldom need any pruning for the first 2 years.

The flowers will develop on short side branches that arise on 2- and 3-year-old canes. In spring, just before the stem buds begin to grow, shorten the side branches to 3 to 6 inches (7.5 to 15 cm) long. Leave three or four buds on each side branch. Also remove any weak, diseased, or dead wood. On older plants, remove one or two of the oldest, dark brown canes each year and train new canes onto the supports.

In summer, remove faded flowers to discourage fruit production and to encourage further flowering on repeat-blooming cultivars, such as 'New Dawn'.

Ramblers

Old-fashioned rambler roses tend to have many clusters of small flowers on long, flexible canes. If you need to manage the growth of a rambler to keep it in bounds, you can remove all of the flowering canes to the ground immediately after they bloom. Then tie the remaining, unbloomed canes to the support.

Part of the charm of a rambling rose is the reckless abandon with which it can cover its supports, old buildings, or trees. For a real low-maintenance approach, let ramblers spread as they will; simply tie in the stems as needed and remove any dead, damaged, or diseased wood as you see it. To encourage heavy flowering on an established rambler, trim back the long side branches to about 6 inches (15 cm) in early spring. Deadheading through the growing season (up to late summer) can keep the flowers coming on reblooming types.

Species Climbers

If you are growing yellow or white Lady Banks rose (*Rosa banksiae*) or similar species climbers, give them plenty of room and little pruning. Shape and train them when they are young. Remove declining canes that are twiggy, congested, or old from more mature plants to keep them vigorous.

Climbing species, like Lady Banks rose, produce long, vigorous canes. Trim mature plants to remove old growth.

Pruning Species and Shrub Roses

In masses for hedges or singly as specimens, species, shrub, and "old" garden roses offer months of beauty with a minimum of maintenance. They need little or no pruning at planting time, except to have dead or damaged wood removed. Once established, most species, shrub, and "old" garden roses benefit from a little light pruning to encourage vigorous new growth.

Species Roses

Species roses include French rose (*Rosa gallica*), rugosa rose (*R. rugosa*), musk rose (*R. moschata*), and Father Hugo's rose (*R. hugonis*), among others. Annually, before spring growth begins, prune lightly to remove dead, diseased, or damaged wood. Also thin out any overly congested or tangled growth. On established plants, remove one or two of the oldest canes at the ground each year to promote vigorous new shoots from the base.

Deadhead the repeat-bloomers so that their energy can go into the next bloom instead of fruit production. On once-bloomers like *Rosa glauca,* skip the deadheading and enjoy the attractive fruits as they form.

Once-blooming Shrub and "Old" Roses

This group includes the albas, centifolias, and moss roses, as well as most damask roses and the modern shrub roses that only bloom once a year. These plants flower mostly on sideshoots from gracefully arching year-old or older canes. Before spring growth begins, shorten the longest canes by up to a third. Trim the side branches

Don't deadhead the spent flowers on rugosa roses or you'll miss the display of showy fruits later in the season.

back to about 6 inches (15 cm). On established plants, prune out one or two of the oldest stems each year.

Reblooming Shrub and "Old" Roses

Included here are the China roses, many of the Bourbons, the repeat-blooming modern shrub roses, and the hybrid perpetuals. These vigorous growers bloom on both the current year's canes and on the sideshoots that form on older canes.

In spring, remove any dead, weak, or poorly placed stems. Prune the longest canes back by no more than one-third to shape the plant and maintain the graceful arching habit. Thin out some of the dense, twiggy growth to keep the center of the plant open to good air circulation. Remove faded flowers to promote more bloom. Prune out one or two of the oldest canes each year on established plants to encourage vigorous growth.

French (Gallica) roses produce many tangled stems. Thin through the season; shorten sideshoots after bloom.

Light, yearly spring pruning is all most established species roses need to look their best and flower freely.

Pruning and Training Annuals and Perennials

A pinch of this and a stake for that—these and other simple steps are the recipe for a neat-looking, flower-filled garden. Use the tips and techniques below to promote sturdier stems and bigger or more abundant blooms throughout the flower garden.

Pinching

Pinching is a quick and easy technique that is useful for many kinds of annuals and perennials. Use it to:

- **Promote bushy growth.** Much like a heading cut, a well-placed pinch removes the stem tip bud. This generally encourages the remaining buds lower on the stem to grow, making the plant fuller.

- **Reduce staking chores.** Pinching also promotes sturdier stems, considerably reducing the need for staking to keep plants upright and looking good.

- **Delay flowering.** The best example is the traditional practice of pinching chrysanthemums to delay flowering until fall. Begin pinching chrysanthemums in spring, and continue about every 2 weeks until July 4 in the South and mid-July in the North. Don't pinch later than that, or your plants may not bloom.

- **Discourage flowering altogether.** Regular pinching can put off flowering on certain plants. This technique is commonly used to promote fresh new growth on herbs such as sweet marjoram, basil, and oregano, which otherwise can become stringy and tasteless once flowering begins. Use the same trick on coleus when you wish to promote the colorful leaves instead of the insignificant flowers.

Pinching out the tips of young plants can promote the production of new shoots, leading to more flowers later.

Pinching Precautions

There are a few situations where pinching may not be helpful. You can't, for instance, depend on pinching to make a plant shorter. Many annuals, perennials, and herbs that are pinched eventually attain the same height they would have had they not been pinched—they're just fuller and sturdier.

Don't pinch plants that send up a single leafy stalk (like lilies) or leafless flowering stalks (like irises). Otherwise, you'll end up taking off the flower buds, and you'll be left with plain stalks sticking up out of the garden.

- **Extend the bloom season.** Extend the bloom time of a mass planting by pinching only half of the plants or by giving half of them one less pinch than the rest. The less-pinched plants will bloom earlier, followed by the more-pinched plants.

The best time to pinch annuals is at planting time. Pinch perennials as they start their spring growth, when there are several sets of full leaves on each stem. Pinch annuals and perennials by taking tip growth away with your thumb and forefinger, normally down to the first full set of leaves below the tip; also pinch away dead or yellow stems or leaves. If the stems are too tough or wiry to break easily with your fingers, use scissors or a sharp pair of pruning shears to make a clean cut.

A midseason pinch works well to keep annuals such as impatiens and begonias from collapsing under their own weight—or flopping under a heavy rain—during a long growing season. Reach about one-third of the way into the plant on each stem and pinch at a joint. The pinched plants may look slightly bedraggled initially. But after a few days, they'll be off and blooming again, only shorter, more compact, and less likely to be damaged during a storm. Do a pinch like this in the early morning or on a cloudy day to keep the tender interior foliage from being scorched. Toss the trimmings in the compost pile, or root them in potting soil to make new plants.

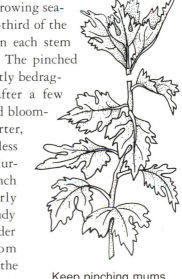

Keep pinching mums up to midsummer and you'll be rewarded with masses of flowers.

You may decide not to deadhead coneflowers, since they produce showy seed heads that can provide winter interest.

Use your fingers or pruning shears to snip spent flowers off cleanly and promote the production of more blooms.

Disbudding

If you are growing carnations, chrysanthemums, dahlias, or peonies, you may want to try this technique for encouraging fewer but larger flowers. Disbudding is easy—simply support the stem gently with one hand and rub or pinch off the unwanted side buds with your other hand. Each disbudded stem will bear one bloom that is larger and showier than normal. Disbudding is not necessarily a technique you'll use regularly, but it's fun to try if you want to have a few special, large blooms for display or use in arrangements.

Deadheading

Deadhead your annuals, perennials, and herbs by pinching off spent flowers. This practice keeps the blooms coming by directing the plant's energy back into more flowers (or into bulb formation) rather than into seed production. Deadheading also prevents plants that self-sow readily—like chives and morning glories—from seeding themselves throughout your garden. Don't use this technique if you *want* to collect the seed or if you are growing the plant for its decorative seed heads.

To deadhead, snap off the faded blooms with your fingers or snip them off with shears. On plants with terminal flowers, pinch the blooms back to a set of full leaves, and you're likely to get additional flowers from the side buds. On plants with flowers that arise on a single leafless stem—including poppies, hostas, pincushion flower (*Scabiosa caucasica*), and most bulbs—follow that stem down to its base and pinch it there.

Disbudding dahlias can give you a few large flowers; keeping all the buds will produce more but smaller blooms.

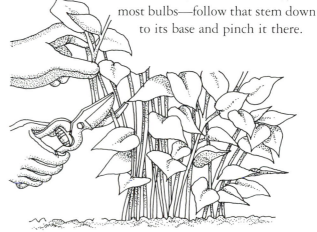

Cut the stalks of faded flowers down to just above a lower leaf or right at ground level.

Cutting aster shoots back by half in early summer promotes sturdier stems and more flowers later in the season.

Cutting Back

Cutting stems back with hand pruners, grass shears, or even string trimmers is a satisfying and worthwhile pruning project that you can do almost anytime.

Fall and Winter Trimming If you like the garden to look tidy over winter, you could cut back all remaining perennials to just above ground level after the first frost. For winter interest, though, you may choose to leave ornamental grasses, evergreen perennials and herbs, and plants with interesting seed heads, like showy stonecrop (*Sedum spectabile*) and coneflowers (*Rudbeckia* spp.). You can wait until late winter to cut these plants back to just above the ground. Make sure you remove the old top growth before spring, or you may end up cutting off some of the new growth as well. If the plants get ratty and you can't stand to look at them, you'll do no harm by cutting them back earlier.

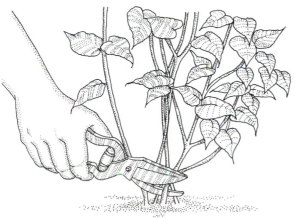

Cut down the stems of flowers after the first frost, or leave them standing until your late winter garden cleanup.

Spring and Summer Trimming Consider cutting back the mat-forming perennials after they bloom. Shearing the stems back by about half will encourage compact growth—and sometimes even a second flush of bloom—on perennial candytuft (*Iberis sempervirens*), wall rock cress (*Arabis caucasica*), moss pinks (*Phlox subulata*), catmints (*Nepeta* spp.), and snow-in-summer (*Cerastium tomentosum*).

Cutting plants back by half in early summer can promote sturdier stems on many tall-growing perennials, including asters, ironweeds (*Vernonia* spp.), great blue lobelia (*Lobelia syphilitica*), and tall native sunflowers (*Helianthus* spp.). Your fall garden will be graced with the later-than-normal flowers, and your plants will resist the temptation to keel over when burdened with all those blooms. Resist the urge to trim tall stems much after early summer, or the plants may not have time to develop new flower buds before frost.

Another great use for cutting back is the old "cut and come again" trick. Shear off the top third of bushy, multistemmed plants after flowering, and you may get another flush of bloom later in the season. Try this on vigorously growing mints, coreopsis (*Coreopsis* spp.), bee balms (*Monarda* spp.), gaura (*Gaura lindheimeri*), and boltonia (*Boltonia asteroides*).

Pinch off faded dahlia flowers as you see them to keep plants looking tidy and blooming freely.

Staking

Staking isn't a particularly low-maintenance approach to plant care, but it doesn't have to take all of your time either. Spend a few minutes in spring to put stakes around the plants you know tend to flop—like peonies and asters—and you'll save yourself the heartache of seeing their beautiful blooms sprawling in the mud after a sudden summer storm.

Bamboo Stakes Bamboo stakes are great for supporting upright, spiky annuals and perennials, such as snapdragons, delphiniums, and foxgloves. Choose stakes that are about two-thirds of the ultimate height of the stem. Place the stakes firmly in the ground when the plants are young, being careful not to insert them through the crowns of the plants. Attach soft fabric or yarn ties to the stakes, then knot the loose ends around the stems as they grow.

Put wire hoops out early so plants can grow up through and cover them.

To support bushy perennials like yarrow and baby's-breath (*Gypsophila paniculata*), place three or four stakes around the clump so that the outer edges of the plant will cover them as the plant grows. String twine back and forth among the stakes to support the stems as they grow.

Pea Brush Pea brush (also called pea staking) is another, far more casual, option for supporting annuals and perennials with slender, floppy stems, like

In the cutting garden, it's not a problem if the staking is visible; it's more important that your flowers are straight.

Cages like linking or ring stakes are easy to install and much more practical than using individual bamboo stakes.

asters (*Aster* spp.) and larkspur (*Consolida ambigua*). It's also a great way to recycle the woody prunings from trees and shrubs. As a precaution, you may want to let the prunings dry out in the sun for a week or so before using them as stakes; if you stick fresh stems into the soil, some might take root!

In early spring, push the stem ends of small twiggy branches firmly into the ground around seedlings, annual transplants, or emerging perennial shoots. The tops of the twigs should be slightly shorter than the ultimate height of the plants they are supporting. As the leaves fill in and the plants approach full size, the staking becomes invisible.

Cages Cages and other wire supports are useful for bushy perennials, like peonies, asters, and Japanese anemones (*Anemone japonica*). Set commercial ring or linking stakes over or around emerging clumps, or make your own supports with pieces of wire-mesh fencing and wooden stakes. Do you find that you're doing entirely too much staking? Check your soil's fertility. Columbines (*Aquilegia* spp.), spiderworts (*Tradescantia* spp.), and other perennials that grow well in lean to moderately fertile soils often grow tall and spindly when given too rich a diet. Hold off on the fertilizer and compost for a year or two.

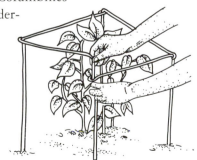

Linking stakes are handy for supporting tall-stemmed annuals and perennials.

Pruning Herbs

Herbs respond generously to pruning. If you give them the best possible growing conditions and pinch them back regularly through the seasons, they will reward you with compact bushy growth and ample harvests for cooking or crafts.

Spring Pruning

Most herbs grow from either the tips (like basil, thyme, oregano, and mint) or from the base (like parsley, sorrel, or chives). At planting time, pinch the tip-growers to encourage growth from the buds lower on the shoot. This will give you a bushier plant and more of those tender, palatable tips.

Trim shrubby herbs, like lavender, sage, southernwood (*Artemisia abrotanum*), hyssop (*Hyssopus officinalis*), and lavender cottons (*Santolina* spp.), back by one-third to one-half to shape them and to encourage the production of new sideshoots.

Summer Pruning

Warm weather will encourage most herbs to grow quickly. Harvest chervil, cilantro, salad burnet, and other herbs that grow from the base by pinching off leaf stalks at ground level around the outside of the clump. This encourages the production of tender new growth in the center of the clump, extending your harvest of tasty leaves.

Through the summer, keep on pinching basil, oregano, mint, and other tip-growing herbs that you are growing for leaves instead of flowers. Shear thyme lightly

Shear lavenders back by one-third to one-half after they bloom to shape the plants and encourage bushy growth.

but often for regular harvests and vigorous regrowth. When possible, pinch or shear in the early morning or on an overcast day; that way, the tender inner leaves will be less prone to damage from sudden exposure to strong sunshine. Use the prunings from culinary herbs in the kitchen, or toss them into your compost pile.

On fast-growing herbs, such as catmints (*Nepeta* spp.) and Roman chamomile (*Chamaemelum nobile*), the foliage can look ratty and tired after flowering. Use the old perennial "cut and come again" trick: Cut them almost to the ground and you'll have fresh late-season foliage and probably another flush of blooms before frost.

Trim and deadhead shrubby herbs like lavender cottons and lavenders by shearing off the top third to half of the stems after bloom.

Rapid growth can cause variegated herbs such as tricolor sage, variegated lemon thyme, and variegated mint to revert to their plain green forms. Pinch away any reverted growth as soon as you spot it. Trimming plants back in midseason can produce a flush of colorful new leaves for the rest of the summer.

Fall and Winter Pruning

At the end of the season, you'll want to cut back all but the evergreen and semi-evergreen herbs (such as lavender, sage, hyssop, and thyme). Gather up the dead top growth and cut it to 1 inch (2.5 cm) or so above the ground with a pair of bypass pruners. Wait until spring to cut back the other herbs. Pick up trimmings and add them to your compost pile.

Cut out dead flowering stems to tidy the garden and give the new leaves more room to develop.

SPECIAL PRUNING PROJECTS

When you have lots to do in the garden and not much time to do it in, the idea of pruning for fun may not sound very appealing. But if you get some extra time and find that the urge to prune is irresistible, the specialized techniques described in this chapter are fun ways to practice your talents. And if you've admired a fanciful topiary or exciting espalier at your local botanical garden, you may be surprised to find out how easy it is to create these special features in your own garden.

Sensitive pruning to create graceful bonsai is a hobby in itself, requiring patience and an understanding of how each plant grows. Specimens that are hundreds of years old fascinate and delight visitors to cultural institutions such as Longwood Gardens, the Arnold Arboretum, and the U.S. National Arboretum. If you are willing to invest the time in training and maintaining bonsai, you can create heirloom specimens to grace your own home and garden.

Espalier—training woody plants to grow flat against a wall or fence—is a less-intensive technique that can add an unusual and dramatic touch to any landscape. If you've got a long, narrow bed between a path and a wall, growing espaliered fruit trees or ornamental shrubs is a great way to make use of this often-ignored space. Espalier-trained trees can also make an attractive and unique fence without taking up much room.

Topiary is another fun and creative way to fine-tune your pruning skills. Over a period of a few years, careful trimming and training can turn a nondescript yew or boxwood into a dramatic spiral, a smooth globe, or a fanciful animal: the possibilities are endless!

This chapter gives you the basics you need to get started with these specialized pruning projects. You'll learn about the techniques involved in each and find suggestions of plants you might like to try the techniques on. With these basics under your belt, you'll be well on your way to a pleasurable and rewarding pruning hobby.

Espalier is a training technique you can use to add charm and beauty to your yard. But espaliers aren't just pretty—they're practical, too; they let you grow fruit trees in narrow spaces that would normally be unproductive.

Basic Bonsai

Bonsai is an art that attempts to replicate, in a container, the look of an old tree that has been shaped by time and the elements. The process of training beautiful bonsai requires time and patience, but the results can be stunning and gratifying.

Caring for Bonsai

Before you buy or begin a bonsai project, be aware that these plants will need some special care. Hardy bonsai normally prefer to be outdoors during the growing season. They enjoy the shelter of a lath house or some other shade-producing structure, where they will receive bright indirect light and protection from the elements. One gust of wind can easily knock over small plants and undo months or years of care!

Bonsai generally grow in shallow pots, so you'll have to water them frequently—possibly as often as twice a day in hot weather—to keep the soil evenly damp. During the winter months, you'll need to protect bonsai from cold temperatures. Many overwinter best in a cool greenhouse, where they will get a dormant, or rest, period. Without this cold period, many hardy plants will not bloom, and they'll gradually become weak and spindly. Bonsai created from houseplants are somewhat easier to care for: They can adapt easily to indoor culture on sunny windowsills or under lights year-round.

Picking a Plant

Generally speaking, the species that adapt best to bonsai training have small leaves, woody trunks, stout limbs, and flowers, fruit, or good fall color. Deciduous plants that make great bonsai subjects include azaleas, beeches (*Fagus* spp.), flowering quinces (*Chaenomeles* spp.), hawthorns (*Crataegus* spp.), ginkgo (*Ginkgo biloba*), Japanese maple (*Acer palmatum*), hornbeams (*Carpinus* spp.), hardy orange (*Poncirus trifoliata*), and zelkova (*Zelkova serrata*). Good choices for evergreens include arborvitaes (*Thuja* spp.), cryptomeria (*Cryptomeria japonica*), boxwoods (*Buxus* spp.), junipers (*Juniperus* spp.), false cypress (*Chamaecyparis* spp.), pines (*P. mugo* and *P. parvifolia*), spruces (*Picea* spp.), and yews (*Taxus* spp.). If you want a bonsai that can grow indoors year-round, consider woody houseplants like serissa (*Serissa foetida*) or weeping fig (*Ficus benjamina*).

When choosing plants for bonsai, consider those that produce showy flowers and fruit as well as attractive foliage.

When choosing a young plant for bonsai, you don't necessarily want a symmetrical, well-balanced specimen. Stems with bends, twists, scars, or stumps can give a bonsai real character; even some dead wood can be desirable! Ask the staff at your local nursery to find out if they have any mangled, misshapen plants that are otherwise destined for the compost pile; with some trimming, these can have immediate impact as bonsai. Of course, potential bonsai specimens should otherwise be healthy and free of insects and disease.

Whatever you pick, just try to start small, with a plant growing in a 1-gallon (4.5 l) or smaller container. If you start with a larger plant, you'll need to root prune it over time, getting the roots into successively smaller pots to control the growth.

Training Bonsai

Choose a shallow pot that looks in scale with the young plant. Cover the drainage holes with a piece of wire screen to ensure good drainage. For soil, use 2 parts potting soil mixed with 1 part leaf mold (screened through a 1/4-inch [6 mm] sieve).

After planting, the next step is to decide what shape you want the plant to grow in. You may allow it to grow upright or encourage a leaning or cascading form. Part of choosing an appropriate style is knowing how a plant grows in its natural setting; books

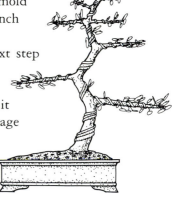

Carefully placed wires help to direct the plant's growth.

Shaping Bonsai

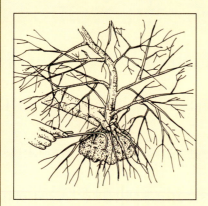

Overgrown plants can have immediate impact as bonsai if well trained.

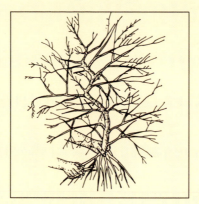

Start by washing off the soil and trimming back the roots.

Prune the top of the plant to reveal the natural branching structure.

with photographs of the plant in the wild may help inspire you. Also consider how your particular plant is growing; it may naturally have a form that suggests a certain shape for easier training.

Pruning, pinching, wiring, and root pruning are standard training techniques you'll use to work with your bonsai. On deciduous plants, do most of your pruning during the dormant season, but don't hesitate to remove undesirable growth as soon as it appears. It's common to remove crossing or rubbing limbs, but you may choose to leave poorly placed branches, depending on the effect you're trying to create. On pines, spruces, and firs, pinch the "candles" (new shoots) back by about half in spring. Carefully trim other evergreens in summer. Pinch any plant through the growing season to direct its growth and to keep it compact.

To shape individual stems, use annealed (softened) #14- to #26-gauge copper wire. Coil the wire gently but firmly over the length of the stem or branch to shape and direct the growth. Check the wire frequently to make sure it isn't cutting into the stem. Take the wire off after several months. To bring upward-pointing branches down to a more horizontal position, use twine or soft string to tie on small weights.

Root pruning is a scary but very necessary aspect of bonsai. It is a key part of keeping the plants in their smaller scale. Do this every 4 to 5 years, in late winter before growth begins for the season, or when you need to repot the plant. Allow the soil to dry slightly more than usual and remove the plant from its pot. Loosen the roots and tease away the soil in the outer third of the root ball. Using thinning cuts, trim away the roots in this outer third. Repot the plant and resume normal maintenance.

If you would like to learn more about the art of bonsai, check out *The Complete Book of Bonsai* by Harry Tomlinson, *Bonsai: The Complete Guide to Art and Technique* by Paul Lesniewicz, or *Bonsai: Step by Step to Growing Success* by Dave Pike.

Display your bonsai creations alone, or group them with other bonsai and container plants in rock gardens. Don't forget to check on them frequently; bonsai need regular watering.

Shaping Espalier

Espalier is a training technique that turns a normally bushy plant into a flat, almost two-dimensional form. Although the technique requires persistent attention and fearless pruning, the results are tremendously rewarding. Use espalier training to cover a blank or nondescript wall, to create a leafy screen that gives privacy to a doorway, deck, patio, or porch or to grow faster-yielding fruit in a small space.

Site and Soil Considerations

Before you choose the plants you want to train, think carefully about the exposure of the site where you plan to create the espalier. In cool and moderate climates, south-facing walls are ideal for sun-loving fruit trees, since the ample light and warmth encourages earlier fruiting and even ripening. In warmer climates, a southern exposure may get too hot, burning the plants or encouraging late-summer growth that is prone to damage from early cold snaps. Western exposures are good for a variety of sun-loving plants. North- and east-facing walls are ideal for shade-loving plants; they also protect evergreens against desiccation and damage from the winter sun and wind.

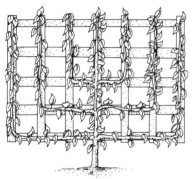

The palmette verrier pattern is popular for apples.

Also keep in mind that soils surrounding fences and walls tend to have built-in difficulties such as compaction, infertility, buried construction debris, sills from building foundations, and alkalinity due to

Espalier training provides you with a good harvest in minimal space. It also makes picking a snap!

leaching from building materials. Try to avoid sites that collect runoff from walkways and driveways where you use deicing salts in winter. (Or use alternative deicing materials, like sand or less-damaging calcium chloride.) Before you plant, do a little digging (and perhaps a soil test) to see what kind of soil conditions you have to work with. Remove any debris you might find, then replace or amend the soil as needed.

Training Styles and Supports

Training styles for espalier are limited only by your imagination. For a classical look, you might choose a formal U-shape, fan, or interwoven Belgian fence pattern. Informal, free-flowing patterns are attractive, too, but they can be more difficult to train without having them look like a jumble of stems.

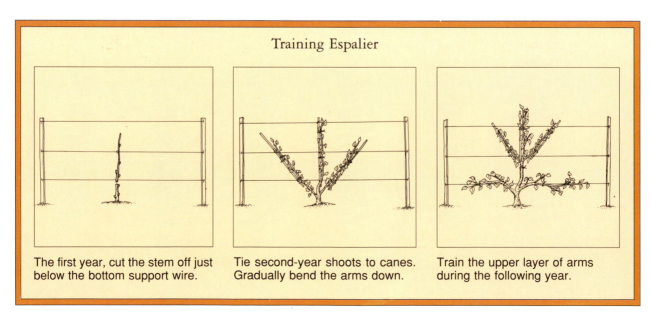

Training Espalier

The first year, cut the stem off just below the bottom support wire.

Tie second-year shoots to canes. Gradually bend the arms down.

Train the upper layer of arms during the following year.

Walls make wonderful supports for espalier-trained trees, but you do need to think carefully before training plants in front of any wall. Painting can become next to impossible as plants fill in, so painted surfaces aren't a good choice; stone, brick, stucco, aluminum or vinyl siding, and unfinished wood seem to be the best options. Also keep in mind that whatever you spray on the plant, you'll spray on the wall, too; pest and disease controls like dormant oil and lime sulfur can discolor some surfaces.

If you do plant against a wall, grow your espalier-trained tree on a wire framework that is at least 6 inches (15 cm) out from the wall. The extra space will make pruning easier and encourage better air circulation around the back of the plant. Attach #10- to #14-gauge, vinyl-covered or galvanized wires to eyebolts coming out from the wall, or string the wires between wooden posts set in front of the wall. Wires strung between posts also make good supports for espalier-trained plants used as fences or screens.

String the first horizontal wire 15 to 18 inches (37.5 to 45 cm) above the ground. Mount additional horizontal wires above this at 15- to 24-inch (37.5 to 60 cm) intervals. Because the plant will eventually acquire some weight and pull down on the wires, turnbuckles are worth their weight in gold to help keep the wires taut. Attach one—fully extended—at the end of each wire you're mounting; plan on tightening it over the years to keep the wires straight.

Plants to Consider

Dwarf fruit trees are popular subjects for this technique. When choosing one, consider that spur-bearing selections—such as pears and many apples—lend themselves well to this method of training because the spurs are long-lived. Tip-bearers such as peaches and plums pose more challenges because you must balance the need for vigorous new growth with the need to control size. On tip-bearers, your annual routine will include the removal of older branches to let new ones take their place—a pretty labor-intensive arrangement. For many fruit trees, you will also need to plant at least two different cultivars to get cross-pollination for good fruit set.

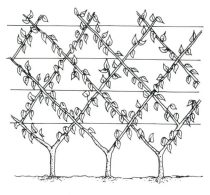

Belgian fence training creates a beautiful living screen.

Other plants worth considering include atlas cedar (*Cedrus atlantica*), sweet bay (*Laurus nobilis*), camellias (*Camellia* spp.), citrus fruits (*Citrus* spp.), cotoneasters (*Cotoneaster* spp.), crabapples (*Malus* spp.), figs (*Ficus* spp.), forsythias (*Forsythia* spp.), ginkgo (*Ginkgo biloba*), hawthorns (*Crataegus* spp.), evergreen magnolias (*Magnolia* spp.), pyracanthas (*Pyracantha* spp.), and flowering quince (*Chaenomeles speciosa*).

If you plan to create a formal espalier, you'll get the best results if you start with a young single-stem tree (commonly known in the nursery trade as a maiden or whip). If you can't find an unbranched tree, at least look for a young plant with an uncut main stem, then trim back the side branches to the main stem. For informal designs, look for a small- to medium-sized plant that already has a pleasing shape; if it already has a somewhat flat habit, so much the better!

Training and Maintenance Techniques

Once your support system is installed and you've chosen a training style, you're ready to plant. Set the new plant about 1 foot (30 cm) in front of the support; this

Atlas cedars and other ornamental trees can be trained to fanciful patterns that add a unique touch to any yard.

A row of espaliered fruit trees makes a pretty and practical divider between the yard and the vegetable garden.

Besides routine pruning and training, fruit trees need a little special attention to give good yields. You'll probably need to do some thinning to get a high-quality harvest of full-sized, well-colored fruit. While fruits are still small, remove any that are damaged or deformed. On plants that will produce large fruit, like apples and peaches, thin the remaining fruits to 6 to 8 inches (15 to 20 cm) apart. Thin smaller fruits, like plums and apricots, to 3 to 5 inches (7.5 to 12.5 cm) apart. If you have to do a lot of thinning, your plant probably has too many fruiting spurs. Remove some, leaving 6 to 8 inches (15 to 20 cm) between spurs.

Some growers root prune their espalier-trained fruit trees to keep them growing compactly and to get them to bear earlier. During the dormant season, use a spade to slice a circle (or half-circle for wall-trained trees) in the soil around the base of the trunk. Make the circle 1 foot (30 cm) in diameter for every inch (2.5 cm) of stem diameter.

will allow plenty of room for the trunk to expand as it grows. If you are growing the plant as a fan or a straight, unbranched stem (called a cordon), tie the main stem or stems to the support wires as they grow.

Patterns that call for horizontal side branches (such as a U-shaped pattern) need more intensive training. Start pruning during the first dormant season after planting or at planting time if your whip is tall enough. Make a heading cut 3 to 4 inches (7.5 to 10 cm) below the first wire; this will cause the stem to branch. Keep three of the new shoots and rub or prune out the rest. Train the center shoot upward to be the central leader. To encourage the "arm" shoots to grow out instead of up, attach them to bamboo stakes, then attach the stakes to the wires. Gradually—over the growing season—move the stakes from the vertical to the horizontal. If you need to bend any stems to form the pattern, do it during the growing season when the stems are about pencil thickness.

Fan training offers a fairly informal look.

As your espalier-trained tree grows, attach the stems you want to keep to the guide wires. Use strong but soft ties, like sisal twine, that will gradually break down. Permanent wire or plastic ties can cut into growing stems and quickly cause permanent damage. Check any ties regularly and replace or add more as needed.

Prune ruthlessly to keep your espalier well shaped. A sharp pair of pruning shears and few basic techniques are all you need to keep an espalier in good form.

- Make thinning cuts to remove awkwardly placed branches, especially those that are growing outward and ruining the two-dimensional effect.
- Use heading cuts where you want a stem to branch or for stopping tip growth when a stem has reached the length you want. During the dormant season (or after flowering for spring-blooming plants), head back side branches on main stems to two or three buds.
- Rub off unwanted shoots and buds before they get large and need to be pruned out. But keep short, blunt, thorn-like fruiting spurs on fruit-bearing plants.

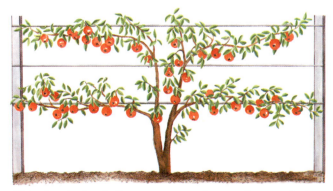

Thin developing fruits on your espaliers so the remainder can mature to full size and ripen evenly.

Training Outdoor Topiary

Training shrubs, trees, herbs, and vines into fanciful shapes is another practice that carries pruning into the realm of sculpture. A single topiary creation can be a graceful or stunning focal point or conversation piece in a small garden; multiple figures can transform a larger space into a magical land peopled with strange and wonderful creatures. If topiary strikes your fancy, the following tips and techniques should help you to further your understanding of this centuries-old art form.

Picking a Plant

Evergreen, small-leaved plants are usually the plants of choice for garden topiary projects. Yews (*Taxus* spp.) and boxwoods (*Buxus* spp.) are traditional favorites. Privets (*Ligustrum* spp.) are inexpensive and grow quickly, but they mostly aren't evergreen and require frequent trimming.

For best results, start with a young or newly planted shrub; older shrubs may require more drastic pruning to get them in the shape you want. If you are buying a shrub for a topiary project from a local nursery, you may want to ask to see any misshapen plants that they can't sell for normal landscaping purposes. A plant with a naturally interesting shape can give your topiary almost immediate interest.

Picking a Pattern

Topiaries are generally trained in either geometric or representational forms. Geometric shapes such as boxes and spheres take less time, thought, and planning, as evidenced by the abundance of such unwitting "topiaries" in residential landscapes. For a more whimsical look, you may shape your topiary into a more unusual form, such as a boat, bird, giraffe, dog, chair, or wishing

> ### For More Tips on Topiary
>
> If you'd like to learn more about the art of creating outdoor and indoor topiaries, check out *The Complete Book of Topiary* by Barbara Gallup and Deborah Reich (Workman Publishing, 1987). It also covers a variety of patterns you can use for shaping espalier-trained trees.

well. If you plan to try a complicated figure, it's helpful to sketch out the final shape you want; then you can refer to the sketch as you prune. Try to keep the figure fairly simple; it can be hard to maintain fine details.

Shaping and Training

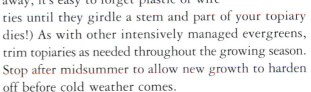

Pruning a topiary involves the same kinds of cuts you use on other landscape plants. Make thinning cuts to remove unwanted growth; use heading cuts to encourage areas to fill in. If you start with small plants, you can train your topiary gradually into its intended form. You may even want to use stakes or bent rods to train key stems into position. (Be sure to attach the stems with twine or some other material that will eventually rot away; it's easy to forget plastic or wire ties until they girdle a stem and part of your topiary dies!) As with other intensively managed evergreens, trim topiaries as needed throughout the growing season. Stop after midsummer to allow new growth to harden off before cold weather comes.

Simple spiral boxwood topiaries add a whimsical touch to this small garden all year long.

Larger topiary projects take time, patience, and lots of trimming, but the results can be worth the effort.

USDA

PLANT HARDINESS ZONE MAP

The map that follows shows the United States and Canada divided into 10 zones. Each zone is based on a 10°F (5.6°C) difference in average annual minimum temperature. Some areas are considered too high in elevation for plant cultivation and so are not assigned to any zone. There are also island zones that are warmer or cooler than surrounding areas because of differences in elevation; they have been given a zone different from the surrounding areas. Many large urban areas are in a warmer zone than the surrounding land.

Plants grow best within an optimum range of temperatures. The range may be wide for some species and narrow for others. Plants also differ in their ability to survive frost and in their sun or shade requirements.

The zone ratings indicate conditions where designated plants will grow well and not merely survive. Refer to the map to find out which zone you are in. In the plant by plant guides, you'll find recommendations for the plants that grow best in your zone.

Many plants may survive in zones warmer or colder than their recommended zone range. Remember that other factors, including wind, soil type, soil moisture and drainage capability, humidity, snow, and winter sunshine, may have a great effect on growth.

Average annual minimum temperature (°F/°C)

Zone 1	Below -50°F/-45°C		Zone 6	0° to -10°F/-18° to -23°C
Zone 2	-40° to -50°F/-40° to -45°C		Zone 7	10° to 0°F/-12° to -18°C
Zone 3	-30° to -40°F/-34° to -40°C		Zone 8	20° to 10°F/-7° to -12°C
Zone 4	-20° to -30°F/-29° to -34°C		Zone 9	30° to 20°F/-1° to -7°C
Zone 5	-10° to -20°F/-23° to -29°C		Zone 10	40° to 30°F/4° to -1°C

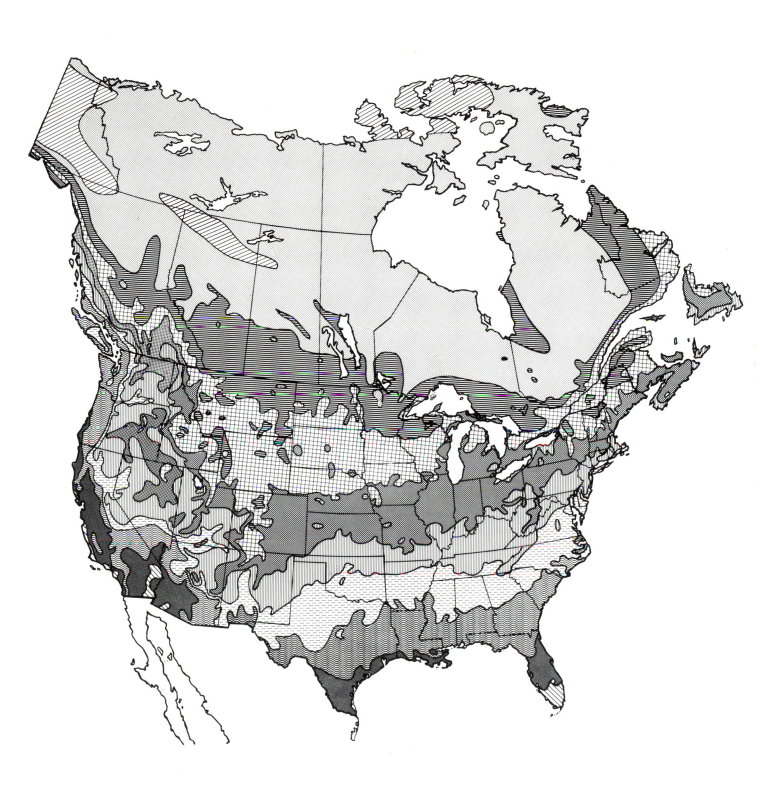

INDEX

The numbers in bold indicate main entries, and the numbers in italic indicate illustrations.

ACKNOWLEDGMENTS

Photo Credits

Heather Angel: pages 61 (bottom), 93 (left), and 135 (left).

A–Z Botanical Collection Ltd: photographer Michael Jones: page 59 (right); photographer M. H. McAndrew: page 125 (left); photographer Maurice Nimmo: page 82 (right); photographer The Picture Store: page 33 (right); photographer Bjorn Svensson: page 86 (bottom).

Gillian Beckett: pages 16 (bottom right), 36 (right), and 44 (right).

Bruce Coleman: photographer Eric Crichton: pages 15 (top), 135 (top right), 143 (bottom), and 150; photographer Dr. Eckart Pott: pages 112 (left) and 114 (top left); photographer Hans Reinhard: pages 103 (top), 106 (bottom), 118 (top), and 140 (top right).

Thomas Eltzroth: pages 96 (left), 98 (left), 99 (left), 104, 107 (left), 119 (top), 121 (left and right), 123 (left), 124 (right), 126 (left), 128 (right), 129 (right), and 130 (left).

Derek Fell: pages 21 (left and bottom right), 22 (bottom), 35 (right), 45 (left), 50 (left), 52 (left), 62, 64 (right), 69 (right), 79 (left), 94 (left), 96 (right), 108 (left and top right), and 115 (bottom).

Garden Picture Library: photographer David Askham: page 18 (right); photographer Brian Carter: page 39 (right); photographer Dennis Davis: page 87 (top); photographer John Glover: pages 23 (right) and 89 (top); photographer Neil Holmes: page 110 (left); photographer Michael Howes: page 110 (bottom right); photographer Lamontagne: pages 18 (left), 30 (top), 63 (left), 151, and 153 (left); photographer Jane Legate: pages 60 (bottom) and 138 (top); photographer Mayer/Le Scanff: page 152; photographer Clive Nichols: page 84; photographer David Russell: page 126 (right); photographer J. S. Sira: page 70 (right); photographer Brigitte Thomas: page 67 (right); photographer Mel Watson: pages 31 and 59 (left); photographer Didier Willery: page 118 (bottom).

Holt Studios International: back cover (center), pages 27 (bottom) and 94 (right); photographer John Adams: page 112 (top right); photographer Richard Anthony: page 131 (right); photographer Nigel Cattlin: pages 15 (bottom), 36 (left), 49 (left), 68 (right), 73 (right), 79 (right), 80 (left), 82 (left), 97 (right), 98 (right), 102 (left), 105, 108 (bottom right), 109 (bottom), 111 (top), 112 (bottom right), 115 (top), 120, 127 (right), 128 (left), 129 (left), and 137 (top); photographer John Henry Galindo: page 122 (left); photographer Irene Lengui: page 60 (top); photographer Rosemary Mayer: pages 29 (bottom) and 102 (bottom right); photographer Primrose Peacock: pages 40 (left), 51 (left), 78 (right), 130 (right), and 132; photographer Inga Spence: pages 100 and 127 (left).

Andrew Lawson: contents page (top left), pages 16 (top right), 57 (top), 88, 90 (bottom), 91 (right), 116 (bottom right), 149, and 153 (center right).

S & O Mathews: pages 30 (bottom), 40 (right), 49 (right), 53 (left), 58, 64 (left), 93 (right), 116 (left), and 136 (bottom).

Clive Nichols: back cover (bottom), half title page, opposite title page, copyright page, pages 8, 11 (left), 12, 14 (bottom left), 17, 21 (top right), 26 (top), 27 (top), 28 (top), 29 (top), 33 (left), 37 (right), 38 (left), 39 (left), 41 (left), 48 (right), 54, 56 (top left), 65 (left), 69 (left), 71 (right), 81 (left), 86 (top), 87 (bottom), 90 (top), 92, 134 (right), 136 (top), 140 (left and bottom right), 142 (top left), and 146.

Jerry Pavia: endpapers, pages 20 (top), 24, and 34 (right).

Photos Horticultural: back cover (top), opposite contents, pages 11 (right), 14 (top right and bottom right), 20 (bottom), 26 (bottom), 41 (right), 46 (right), 57 (bottom), 61 (top), 67 (left), 70 (left), 72 (right), 73 (left), 77 (right), 81 (right), 83 (right), 89 (bottom), 91 (left), 102 (top right), 106 (top), 107 (right), 109 (top), 110 (top right), 111 (bottom), 114 (bottom left), 116 (top right), 117 (top and bottom), 119 (bottom), 125 (right), 134 (left), 135 (bottom right), 137 (bottom), 138 (bottom), 139 (top), 141, 142 (bottom left), 143 (top), 144 (top and bottom), 145 (top and bottom), and 148.

Harry Smith Collection: front cover, pages 16 (bottom center), 22 (top), 28 (bottom), 32, 34 (left), 43 (left and right), 44 (left), 46 (left), 47 (right), 48 (left), 51 (right), 53 (right), 65 (right), 66 (right), 68 (left), 71 (left), 72 (left), 74 (left and right), 76 (left and right), 78 (left), 80 (right), 97 (left), 103 (bottom), 114 (right), 122 (right), 123 (right), 124 (left), 131 (left), 139 (bottom), and 153 (bottom right).

Weldon Russell: photographer John Callanan: pages 35 (left), 37 (left), 38 (right), 42 (left and right), 45 (right), 47 (left), 50 (right), 52 (right), 63 (right), 66 (left), 75 (left and right), 77 (left), 83 (left), 95 (left and right), 99 (right), and 142 (right); photographer David Wallace: title page, contents page (bottom left and right), pages 23 (left) and 56 (center left).